Heartland Strong

How rural New Zealand can change and thrive ———

Heartland Strong

Edited by Margaret Brown, Bill Kaye-Blake and Penny Payne

MASSEY UNIVERSITY PRESS

Contents

The Wairoa River, in northern Hawke's Bay. Beautiful landscapes and natural recreational assets, such as rivers, are seen by locals as some of the benefits of living in rural communities.

Rural towns are central to the resilience of
New Zealand's agricultural communities. The
general store at Ongaonga has been trading
since 1899.

Introduction

The future of New Zealand's rural communities is unclear. Empty shops, depopulation and lack of jobs are all offered as signs that many towns are dying. However, the strength of social ties and development of digital technologies, the innovations in rural entrepreneurship and the functioning informal economy suggest that some rural communities are in good health.

As researchers, we wanted to know what people in these towns thought about their own resilience, so we went and asked them. In 2016 we held a series of workshops in several small North Island towns and asked residents how their communities were doing. To some extent, what they said wasn't surprising. They pointed to businesses and government offices that had closed, to environmental issues that needed addressing, to schools and clubs that didn't have enough members, and to difficulties accessing services such as healthcare, post offices and banks.

At the same time, they talked about what they did have. They had good schools with excellent staff. They had natural resources such as rivers, lakes and bush for locals and tourists to use. They spoke of strong Māori culture with proud whakapapa and diverse iwi. Most of all, they talked about living in places where they knew people on the street and could stop for a natter and a cuppa. They identified strong rural communities and a sense of belonging.

Those discussions suggested an underlying resilience that isn't captured in some of the ongoing debates about the future of rural communities. They also echoed some of the research that the authors of this book have been undertaking for the past 10 years or more. Our research has investigated resilience on farms and in communities, as well as the links between the two. We thought it was time, therefore, to summarise what we have learned.

There are many definitions of resilience. In our research, we define it as *the ability of a social system to adapt.* This does not necessarily mean adapting to return to the way things were; it can also mean transformation and renewal within a community. In this way, we see disturbances to rural communities as sometimes negative, but also as opportunities for positive change.

While most resilience literature has focused on natural disasters or traumatic events, this book looks more at adaptation to gradual change, such as the depopulation of rural areas. This approach to resilience means we consider it to be a) ongoing, b) both positive and negative, and c) part of a wider system change.

We see this book as a part of a conversation with other writers and researchers who are interested in rural communities. We also think it fills gaps in the New Zealand literature on the resilience of rural communities. Some examples may help.

Economist Shamubeel Eaqub led New Zealanders to talk about 'zombie towns' — towns that won't die but are left to shuffle along as people and businesses leave.[1] He raised provocative questions: should New Zealand have an active policy of putting 'dying' towns out of their misery? How much responsibility does the rest of the country have for towns that no longer serve a clear function?

Massey University's Paul Spoonley undertook research on shifting demographics and the inevitable impacts on New Zealand regions.[2] As he pointed out, changes are already largely locked in: future demographics are mostly the result of past birth patterns and the passage of time. The expected result is fewer people in rural areas, with many of them being older.

These two examples show how the New Zealand literature tends not to explore the elements that make for vibrant or successful rural communities and tends to focus on one topic at a time: economics or demography or the environment. Our approach is to consider economics *and* demography *and* the environment, aiming for a holistic description of rural communities.

There is no getting away from the pressures, drivers and trends that are challenging the rural sector. The view popularised by Eaqub and Spoonley is that these trends will ultimately bring about the end of parts of rural New Zealand.

An alternative perspective

There is another view, however. Rural areas represent the bulk of the land mass of New Zealand, and therefore the bulk of its natural resources. These areas contribute significantly to the economy and have been growing in productivity. Rural communities contain quite a few of New Zealand's people — families and organisations who contribute to the social and cultural make-up of the country. Many of our rural communities represent what New Zealanders love about their country. They are friendly and tight-knit and provide a place to reconnect with the rural environment — the rivers, the mountains, the small-town New Zealand feel. Rural areas also have a large proportion of tangata whenua, as well as their physical resources: marae, culture and tūrangawaewae (places to stand). Rural communities have shown themselves to be resilient over many years; that is likely to continue.

Based on many years of working with rural communities, we wanted to emphasise several aspects. Most importantly, people in rural communities, whether living in townships or not, do have options.

On farm, there have been a lot of changes over the past 20 years and farmers continue to adapt and innovate. A few key facts summarise some of the changes. The number of sheep in New Zealand has fallen from more than 70 million in 1982 to almost 28 million in 2016, a decline of around 60 per cent. Nevertheless, the amount of sheep meat exported from the country has barely changed. Farmers have learned to produce roughly the same amount of meat from less than half the number of animals. The production techniques have changed accordingly, and Chapter 1 describes some of the differences, including the impacts of irrigation and intensification. There is also significant interest in new crops and new techniques.

Farmers have expanded into entrepreneurial businesses, as described in Chapter 11, including niche, value-add farming operations. Examples include organic farms, tourist-destination farms and farm-level diversification. Farmers are demonstrating adaptability in the face of a changing economic, social, environmental and cultural scene in New Zealand. In fact, the New Zealand Productivity Commission found that the primary sector, including agriculture, had the highest rate of labour productivity growth of any sector since 1985 and was above average between 2000 and 2011.

It is also important to recognise that people are resilient. People exercise some control over their lives, something psychologists and sociologists call 'agency'. They make choices and strive to do as well as they can. Language that focuses on 'zombie towns' has the side effect of making the residents seem like victims. Similarly, focusing on demographic trends can threaten to turn people into bystanders.

When we talk to people in rural areas, they are well aware of the challenges they face and can make a list of them as well as anyone. However, they also know that the rural economy has ups as well as downs and that they have collective social capital to draw on when necessary. Chapter 4 describes what happened when the floods hit

Manawatū in 2004. Many farmers initially managed the effects on their farms and rallied to help their neighbours get up and running in the short term. They then took the opportunity to work out how to manage their properties better, leading to the Sustainable Land Use Initiative. Farmers worked with Horizons Regional Council to create balanced farm plans that encouraged them to retire challenging terrain and focus on the productive parts of their farms. The result was improved environmental resilience because of less erosion from steep land.

Resilience is complex

These communities continue to function partly because resilience isn't just about jobs or ageing populations or environmental impacts or social connections; it's a combination of these things, in ways that aren't fully understood. This notion is supported by research in Wairoa, in Hawke's Bay, as discussed in Chapter 2. Wairoa has several indicators of vulnerability: few jobs and low incomes, and the recent closing of one of its supermarkets. Our research showed, however, that its informal economy is strong and contributes significantly to people's well-being.

One last thing to point out about resilience: it is more than local — it is 'local and larger'. We see this repeatedly with policies that operate at both the national and the local level. One example is freshwater policy. The aim and the direction of the policy were set at the national level, with the National Policy Statement for Freshwater Management. The statement starts with objectives about safeguarding the life-supporting capacity of water and enabling communities to provide for their economic well-being. By the end of that very same page, the national-level statement describes how the objectives will be achieved: 'By every regional council making or changing regional plans to the extent needed to ensure the plans'. All such national-level policies require regional-level change, so the well-being of the regions depends partially on national-level policies. In addition, achieving overall goals for the country depends on having regional communities that are resilient enough to contribute to those goals.

When we held workshops in rural communities, as detailed in Chapter 3, the participants were well aware of the interaction between local resilience and decisions made elsewhere. In Taumarunui, for instance, participants talked about the decision made by KiwiRail to cancel the regular stop at the town, and the impacts on residents and tourism. Across the communities, residents talked about central government facilities that were once located in the regions and had since been shifted to cities. They pointed out that these decisions, which are made to help the ministries and state-owned enterprises and their employees, result in hurting the towns that are left behind. Local residents are clear that they have to contend not just with the impacts of local decisions on their resilience but also with the impacts of decisions made far from their communities.

A bit about us

The authors of this book are researchers focused on agriculture and rural communities. There are two things we would like you to know about us.

The first is that we come from different specialities. The social researchers have backgrounds in rural sociology, community development, education, geography and economics. The physical scientists have backgrounds in ecology, farm systems, animal nutrition and more. This allows us to take different perspectives on the same issue. That's important, because a problem in a rural community is never 'just' an economic problem or a social problem or an environmental problem. More to the point, the solution to a problem is never simply from one speciality or another. An environmental problem may have a technical solution, but that solution needs to fit within the farm management methods being used and the economics of the operation. Solutions must also be socially feasible. If a solution is technically accurate but farmers will not implement it, it is not really a solution.

This brings us to the other important thing about our team: we have figured out how to work together as an interdisciplinary team. Gabriele Bammer, a professor at Australian National University, has researched interdisciplinary teams and wrote an influential book on the topic.[3] She found that learning to work together is one of the biggest challenges of interdisciplinary research. Disciplines have different sets of priorities and assumptions; they use different language and techniques and they can be difficult to understand from the outside. Learning to work beyond those difficulties and share knowledge without 'dumbing it down' has been part of developing our research team. Indeed, one member of our team researches interdisciplinary teams and uses us as subjects for that research. We don't always get it right, but we have had some successes with our approach that make us keen to continue.

This book is based primarily on our work in two projects that have been running consecutively since 2007: Rural Futures and Resilient Rural Communities. Rural Futures was originally funded through New Zealand's competitive funding system by the Foundation for Research, Science and Technology (FRST). Later, funding for the two programmes came from AgResearch's core funding and has also become part of the Our Land and Water — Toitū te Whenua, Toiora te Wai National Science Challenge. AgResearch has been the lead organisation over that whole period and has involved Lincoln University, the University of Otago, and several other organisations and independent researchers. More than 30 researchers have been involved in the work.

Rural Futures focused on supporting the New Zealand pastoral industry to adapt and remain sustainable in response to the future pressures it faced. Those pressures haven't really changed in the more than 10 years since the programme was conceived. Farmers are working to compete in global markets, where a combination of prices, consumer demands and supply chain requirements continues to challenge them. Societal and policy changes that operate at local, national and international levels create additional demands for farmers on how they operate and how they measure and manage the effects of these changes. The agricultural sector also faces several constraints. Energy, soil, water and skilled labour are vital to agriculture but are also limited. New Zealand farmers and the agents who advise them must learn, plan and innovate around these constraints. Rural Futures therefore focused on developing tools, processes and systems to help farmers, advisors and industry groups respond to risks and opportunities in ways that are environmentally, economically and socially sustainable.

Resilient Rural Communities has shifted that focus a little. It started from the perspective that farms need rural communities and those communities need healthy farms. It seeks to understand the drivers of community resilience, and to help communities improve this resilience. There is also a strong mātauranga Māori (Māori knowledge) component in our resilience research.

An important part of Resilient Rural Communities is outreach to stakeholders in the rural sector. It is working to create connections to people and organisations who have stakes in rural community development, in order to ensure that the research is useful and relevant. That makes it both a research programme and an extension programme — an unusual combination in this country. The focus is on the widest group of stakeholders possible: farmers, rural residents, social and community groups, local and central government, industry groups, rural businesses and allied businesses such as banks and agribusiness suppliers.

A bit about this book

This book takes what we have learned about rural community resilience to a wider audience. We have published academic papers and reports over the past decade, for which the references and links can be found on our website.[4] We have engaged less with the public about our science — until now. Throughout this book, we explain the technical aspects of our research and show how it is relevant to rural communities and New Zealand generally.

The book is divided into four sections. The first section outlines key changes in agriculture over the past 20 years. It then describes a few rural communities in New Zealand in which we have undertaken research. The aim of the section is to make these places and changes real for the reader. The second section moves away from specific places into general concepts; it presents the frameworks we have been using to guide our research. It also describes some of the tools we use to amass a broad range of information and make it understandable.

The second half of the book is more forward-looking. Section Three considers different drivers of change and how they might affect rural areas. The drivers include Māori tino rangatiratanga (self-determination) in their tūrangawaewae, increasing environmental pressures on farming, and future technologies that are changing all of society. Section Four then returns to the idea of integration. It considers how agriculture and its connections to the environment and communities could be managed in the future, from both Māori and Pākehā perspectives.

In the concluding chapter, we come back to the idea of visiting the countryside. This time we consider what might change in the future and the impacts on communities' resilience. The conclusion also considers the role that people's decisions could play in creating a resilient future.

We have written this book for a wide range of people with an interest or a stake in resilient rural communities: the people who live there, the businesses that operate there, local and national government and, ultimately, New Zealanders in general. We hope it provides useful insights into the ongoing process of change in rural communities and the resources on which they draw to support their resilience.

1. What is happening within New Zealand's rural communities?

Dairy cows, Canterbury. The strength of the dairy export market has meant a dramatic growth in dairying, with consequent changes in on-farm practices.

1.

Chapter 1 —

On-farm changes that have affected rural communities in the past 20 years

— *Margaret Brown and Penny Payne*

This chapter takes you on a drive through the New Zealand countryside to see just how much our farms and communities have changed over the past couple of decades.

Changing landscape, changing labour

Today you will see dairy cows on land that 20 years ago would have been sheep and beef country: there are large numbers of dairy cows in Canterbury, Southland and, to a lesser degree, Northland. As dairy cow numbers have grown, sheep have decreased in number as they are pushed back on to the less profitable, harder-to-farm hill country. Dairy expansion has brought increases in the total number of herds, the sizes of existing herds and the number of larger herds.[1]

There has also been enormous growth in water storage systems and the use of irrigation. Today a drive across Canterbury will take you past large storage ponds and irrigation canals that move water across country from rivers to storage ponds and tanks, and you won't fail to notice the large number of irrigators marching across the countryside. The increased use of irrigation has enabled farmers to intensify their production systems and raise crops that could not have been grown in these areas 20 years ago. All these changes have affected our rural communities.

The intensification of farming in many parts of New Zealand over the past 20 years has resulted in an increased demand for services on farm and off farm to support the growing industry. These demands have affected rural communities both positively and negatively. More intensive farm systems often require more people to work on the farms. Finding and retaining 'good' workers on farms has become an increasing problem over this time. Twenty years ago, there was still a healthy pool of young New Zealanders who wanted to work on farms and perhaps work their way up to farm ownership. Now that pool has dried up considerably, and the agricultural industry has increasingly had to bring in immigrant labour to fill these positions.

More people living and working on farm means an increased demand for community services, such as health, education and recreation. The growth of the dairy industry also means that the labour force has become more transient because the length of contracts is in many cases only a few years. This movement of people results in peaks and troughs in the demands for education and health services, in particular. Small rural communities have found it increasingly difficult to accommodate these ups and downs in demand, so many services have moved from these communities and consolidated in larger rural towns.

The Canterbury Plains, traditionally a region of sheep farming and cropping, has been changing in recent years as irrigation has allowed dairying to become an option for many farmers.

This move to larger centres results in a 'hollowing out' of smaller settlements. This is evident when you drive through many small rural towns today and you see that the shop, garage, trucking company and church have all closed. On your travels you will also see a considerable number of closed schools. Some of these will have been consolidated into a neighbouring school, and others will have been closed completely.

Intensification in farming and the use of more high-tech technologies on farm has also increased the demand for off-farm services such as building, repairs and maintenance, and contracting. As farms have increased in size and intensification, many farm owners have opted not to own machinery for jobs such as ground work and forage sowing because of the high cost of owning, operating and maintaining specialist machinery. This has contributed to an increased demand for agricultural contracting services.

The increase in jobs both on and off the farm has led to fewer people in some rural communities and more people in other, now larger, rural communities. That is, we have seen the loss of small satellite rural communities; for example, people and resources moving from Aria and Piopio to Te Kūiti. For the people living and working on farm, this can mean more time travelling to access essential services, such as school, shops and medical centres, or having to limit the use of these services.

The intensification of farming is not all negative, though. A drive today through the countryside in the South Island will take you through many towns that have flourished on the growth and intensification of farming. One notable example is Ashburton. Twenty years ago it was a quiet rural service town, and today it is a larger, bustling, vibrant town. Another example in the South Island is Timaru, which has grown and flourished on the expansion and diversification of agriculture in the area. This trend is good for the larger rural towns and provides a type of consolidation of resources for the region, as the broader population is enough to sustain the town's growth.

Increase in regulation and compliance: Society's demands

Continue to drive through the rural landscape, and up the drive on to any type of farm and you will most likely be confronted by a medley of attention-grabbing signs on the gates and sheds alerting you to all kinds of hazards and actions required of you as a visitor. You will likely also be asked to sign in and listen to a safety briefing; because of the *Mycoplasma bovis* issue, you may also have to walk through a footbath, scrub your boots and possibly hose down your vehicle before driving on to the farm.

And these are only the requirements for visitors. On farm, the farmer will be actioning a plethora of regulation and compliance requirements every day of the week. For example, they will be carrying out and monitoring health and safety regulations; animal welfare regulations; chemical and prescription medicine handling regulations; and water quality requirements, such as the fencing and planting of riparian strips on some streams. They will also be recording animal movements for traceability while putting practices into their farm systems to lower their environmental impact and possibly also their greenhouse gas emissions.

Today's farmer must farm with many more regulations and standards set beyond the farm gate than their counterparts of two decades ago. As one young farmer said recently, 'We haven't got time to actually farm; we are too busy filling out forms and paperwork [to meet compliance requirements].'

Along with an increase in regulation and compliance requirements, the past 20 years have seen an increase in pressures and demands from New Zealand society and overseas consumers. New Zealand farmers once farmed in relative 'splendid isolation'. That is, they farmed primarily to meet their own family and business goals, guided by their sector organisations and market signals, and by some central and local government regulations; beyond these influences, farming was largely unaffected. But this has changed markedly, driven by such factors as the degradation of river water quality, rising interest in the environmental footprint of agriculture, and consumers' interest in where their food comes from and the standard of animal care that takes place in the production of their food.

These requirements reflect the growing gap between a broad public desire for farming to be clean, ethical and honest and some of the perceived realities of modern-day farming in New Zealand. Research suggests that people want to know that traditional farming — such as contact between the animal and the farmer, greenery being provided for livestock, calves and cows kept together, and animals grazing on real grass — is still occurring.[2] This same research also suggests that those who have lived or worked in the country or agricultural sector have a greater understanding of what modern-day farming requires.

These findings suggest that continued communication between rural and urban communities is critical for bridging the gap in understanding. The pressure from urban consumers also suggests that, despite the technological revolution that is bringing robotic milking and synthetic foods, there is still a place for traditional family farms in New Zealand.

Farm ownership changes

Farm ownership structures have also been changing over the period in question. While the family farm is still the dominant ownership model today, there has been tremendous growth in corporate and syndicate farm ownership systems. Twenty years ago, the dream of owning a farm was still a possibility for young people who were prepared to work hard. For example, in the dairy industry, young farmers could work their way to farm ownership through a series of management and share-milking positions. This is still possible today, but it has become increasingly difficult to do. The price of cows and land has increased steadily, making the purchase of both out of reach of most young farmers without some form of financial assistance beyond the banks.

Accordingly, the farm owner in many cases is no longer one family but increasingly a group of investors or a corporate owner of some description.[3] These arrangements include equity partnerships, interest from foreign ownerships and leasing. These forms of farm ownership provide initial financial investment to set up the farm, but also mean investors want regular returns on their investments. When prices for milk or meat fall, or there is a severe weather event, corporate farms are not as able as the family farm to 'hunker down', reduce spending and ride out the low period. The average age of a farm owner has increased over the past 20 years from 56.5 to 58 years old.[4] This trend is coinciding with a 23.5 per cent decrease in the average number of farms in New Zealand between 2002 and 2016.[5] Also, the farms that continue to exist tend to be larger.

Whereas 20 years ago many farming families would have a successor to take over the farm when the parents were in their fifties to sixties, farm succession is now a major issue for many farming families.[6] Back then, it was common for one child in the family, usually a son, to take over the farm when the parents reached retirement age. Today, fewer children in farming families want to become farmers or work in agricultural industries. There are a host of reasons for this: more young people want to move to the cities for higher-paying jobs or occupations; different parental expectations, meaning less pressure from parents on their children to be farmers; and active discouragement from some farming parents because they see farm ownership as increasingly complex and financially risky. In addition, many young people don't want to take on large debt and work the long hours. These changes have had a profound effect on rural communities, including a resultant population decline.

Weather: More extreme events

As if these changes were not enough of a challenge for rural communities the weather has also been changing over the past 20 years and is likely to continue doing so for the next 20. There has been a noticeable rise in the number of severe weather events to hit the countryside. In 2017 there was an increase in rainfall of between 120 and 149 per cent for Auckland, Waikato, Bay of Plenty and other regions, while Southland and Otago had only 50 to 79 per cent of the average annual rainfall.[7] The year 2017 was also the fifth-warmest on record, with six months of the 12 being above the average temperature by up to 2.4°C.

There have always been snowstorms, floods and droughts, but the number, frequency and intensity of these events have been increasing, with often devastating effects on rural communities. Twenty years ago, storms such as Cyclone Bola, which hit the East Coast of New Zealand in 1988, were rare events that made media headlines because of the destruction they caused on farms, which in turn affected the off-farm services provided by the rural communities in the district.

Now extreme events — such as the 2018 storm that caused devastation to the Tolaga Bay region after washing forestry 'slash' (rubbish left after logging) down on to farmland and into rivers — make media headlines, but they are neither rare nor unusual. Severe weather events that affect farmland often affect rural communities because farmers have less need, temporarily, for some off-farm services. They may have less spending money, which in turn may mean jobs in rural communities are lost and people are forced to move away.

Looking forwards

Our drive through the countryside and review of the past 20 years has shown many changes, from more dairy farms and an increase in commercial farming operations to increased compliance and a more extreme climate. These changes demonstrate that farming and rural communities need to cultivate the five types of resilience — social, cultural, economic, environmental and organisational — to make it through.

The following chapters explore rural resilience and what it means to different people. You will see on-the-ground examples of building resilience in our communities today, how things are changing, and how rural communities are adapting to these changes. This book provides tools that will help rural communities plan for and cope with the changes so that they can not only bounce back — they can also bounce forwards.

Chapter 2 —

Wairoa: Resilience and change

— *Willie Smith*

Set along the banks of the Wairoa River, the township of Wairoa has substantial appeal. The surrounding district stretches inland to the beautiful, steep hill country that runs up to Te Urewera, also known as the Urewera Ranges. Lake Waikaremoana lies 60 kilometres to the north-west. The Wairoa district's coastal margins offer access to rich fishing grounds and provide popular recreational and tourist facilities. Its areas of steep land are susceptible to erosion and it has less flat, alluvial land than is common elsewhere in the North Island. The climate is notable for its variability and the frequency of storms.

The rate of change in the Wairoa district has left it lagging behind other parts of the Hawke's Bay region and New Zealand as a whole. The population of the district has declined by 6.9 per cent since 2006, from 8481 to 7890. The hourglass structure of the population has become more marked: there are disproportionate numbers of children, young people and elderly people. The percentage of residents in full-time employment has fallen and the number of unemployed has increased.

These trends are long-standing and serve as a barometer of the challenges faced by the community. The Wairoa District Council has worked since at least the late 1990s to reverse the trends and increase the resilience of the district,[1] and the council enjoys strong community support. In the 2013 local body elections, Wairoa achieved a 62 per cent turnout, while the nationwide rate was 48 per cent.[2]

This chapter examines resilience through the lens of Wairoa. It draws on evidence from descriptive statistics and research findings, as well as the voices of residents in workshops and interviews and through local activities. These activities include voluntary work found in the district, such as the annual Wairoa A&P Show and the weekly farmers' market.

This case study finds that resilience in Wairoa is complex. In the short to medium term, it is closely linked to changes in land use. Long-term resilience, however, hinges on issues of capacity, power and scale that directly impact upon the resilience of human systems.[3]

Farm–community links and the resource base

Today the Wairoa district remains predominantly agricultural, although forestry has increased and is projected to continue growing. Land use and land-use changes have fundamental implications for employment and the linkages between the rural hinterland and the township.

This is not a one-way street. Farm households have traditionally used their local town centres as sources of labour and supplies; urban residents have used farms as sources of employment. Good times on the farm generate spending in local settlements; hard times bring retrenchment.

This is highlighted by the massive decline in the financial well-being of farmers in the post-1984 period that followed the withdrawal of farm subsidies, which affected rural businesses. Between 1984 and 1988 employment in the New Zealand fertiliser and agricultural equipment sectors declined by 48.8 per cent and 51.2 per cent respectively, while capital expenditure by farmers fell from $300 million to $100 million.

Although other factors were also at play, the loss of shops and service depots in many small towns was the most visible evidence of the rural crisis at that time. Similar repercussions are evident today in many small towns, whether in the face of drought or other events that result in a downturn in farm income and farm spending.

Farm–community linkages in the context of land use and social change are long established as components in the resilience of small towns.[4] A New Zealand study confirms this view,[5] but also demonstrates that changes in such linkages are now complex and multifaceted. They are a result not only of domestic policy shifts but also of structural changes in traditional economic and social relations.[6]

Farmer opinion reinforces the continued importance of farm–community links. It also reinforces an almost unanimous belief that the hollowing out of rural communities — whether in terms of a decline in policing and recreational facilities (and sports teams) or the closure of local schools, health facilities and retail services — is the greatest risk to their resilience on the land. Similar conclusions are confirmed in overseas experience.

Such findings set Wairoa centre stage in the ongoing global debate on rural change and resilience. They strengthen the perspective that it is 'place' (and people in that place), rather than sectoral policies, that determines resilience. This confirms the view that sectoral policies for agriculture on their own cannot ensure rural revitalisation and development.[7] In effect, it is strong rural communities that are essential for agricultural transition and renewal.

Rural events such as Wairoa's A&P show are a
significant element in rural community support
and engagement systems.

Bridging the formal and informal economy

Farming in the Wairoa district has also changed, in line with national and international trends. While agricultural land in the district is still used overwhelmingly for sheep and beef (98 per cent), the number of farms has decreased (from 454 in 1990 to 330 in 2017), the average farm size has increased and stock numbers have fallen.

Shifts in farm specialisation have also occurred and traditional farm–community links have changed. Not all livestock raised is processed locally at the single meat-processing plant in Wairoa. Some stock is moved out of the district due to farmer loyalty, price competition or other factors. With no wood-processing plant in the district, raw timber continues to be moved out of the area for export through Gisborne and Napier. Farm labour demands have decreased and farm input supplies may now be sourced from more distant centres. This hollowing out of rural facilities has also altered traditional rural–urban relationships.[8]

These statistics suggest that Wairoa is in decline. A sole reliance on such indicators, however, encourages a focus only on those components that are easily measurable. Job creation is unquestionably fundamental to public and district council concerns: jobs retain and attract people to the district. There is equally a need to maintain necessary public facilities. Yet resilience and well-being involve the mutual influences between material capital (including natural resources and the environment) and human capital (including communities' self-belief, positivity, leadership and experience).[9] It is these primary characteristics that allow communities facing apparent decline to grow.

In June 2016 community members, including young Māori farmers, business people and other residents, gathered for an AgResearch workshop in Wairoa. They discussed their vision for their community. They also discussed the strengths, weaknesses and opportunities facing the district. What stood out was the enormous commitment to Wairoa's growth and success, and the belief that the fundamental strength of the district lies in its social cohesion, backed by a good district council.

Workshop participants reiterated the need for job opportunities, but they also highlighted Wairoa's social factors and the lifestyle they enjoy. They expressed the unanimous opinion that 'it is a great place to live'. Their views focused attention on a particular fact about Wairoa: participation in the voluntary economy is 21.8 per cent, significantly higher than the average in New Zealand (13.9 per cent), and it has stayed constant since 2001, while the national average has fallen.[10]

The informal economy (or voluntary work) used to be associated with underdevelopment and backwardness. As development increased, the informal economy was assumed to shrink and disappear.[11] Evidence from both the developing and developed world counters this view; there is a blurring of the formal/informal divide and an interdependence of both components. The informal economy is now recognised as a global phenomenon that persists, adapts and contributes to changing needs, including sustainability, resilience, innovation and entrepreneurship, rural development and natural resource use. It is also recognised as a means of ensuring cultural and social survival and well-being.

The informal economy is defined in different ways but centres on voluntary activities.[12] Stats NZ defines these as unpaid activities performed for people living in the same household or outside the household. It does not include illegal activities but does include household and carer work and child-minding.[13] Using this definition, AgResearch carried out a survey of 39 voluntary workers in Wairoa in 2017. The aim was to understand their characteristics, the reasons for their involvement and the benefits they gained or sought. This included the Māori contribution, which extends well beyond this one cultural group. A specific component of the exercise, however, addressed the role of the informal economy in Māori culture and the resilience of the Māori community.

Sharing, volunteering and mutual support are viewed as inherent

The Wairoa A&P show is an important date in the local community calendar. Similar A&P shows, and other regular events around the country, are key to maintaining the social networks vital to rural resilience.

characteristics of being and as central elements in Māori identity.[14] Research confirms the importance of the voluntary sector to Māori; it is celebrated and a source of pride. The roots of Māori involvement and the importance of the voluntary sector to Māori have been explored in some depth and have parallels among other indigenous peoples.[15] One Māori respondent in Wairoa explained her participation in work on her marae simply by saying, 'It is a vital part of being kāinga [home].'

Domestic responsibilities are a significant part of voluntary work in Wairoa. Of those surveyed, 17.3 per cent looked after a child who was not a family member. The national average is 13.7 per cent. Similarly, 11.2 per cent looked after someone who was ill or disabled, compared with a national average of 7.9 per cent.

This high level of commitment to domestic responsibilities transcends any cultural divide. Thus, while the high level of what might be described as 'necessary volunteering' may be linked to the presence of so many low-income households and a lack of alternative paid employment, many of those interviewed obtained satisfaction from their domestic work, a feature also identified in the UK.[16] As in the UK, respondents in Wairoa also noted that there was difficulty in accessing quality paid assistance.

The importance of organisational voluntary work is highlighted by the 70 local social clubs and associations found in Wairoa District,[17] ranging from Scottish country dancing to pottery, sailing, rugby, hunting and tennis. These groups were widely acknowledged by participants in the June 2016 workshop as making a major contribution to the quality of life their families enjoy.

In a district with fewer than 8000 residents, some of these clubs are small, but their number and range are significant. Many individuals also make major unpaid contributions to the A&P Show, the weekly farmers' market and similar events. The work and initiative of the Wairoa Centennial Library, demonstrated in their school holiday reading programme for children, is a notable example.

The time commitment of volunteers is difficult to assess. The survey in Wairoa suggests that volunteering ranges from what amounts to full-time employment to a substantial commitment on top of full-time, paid work. A study in 2014 estimated that the value of unpaid care alone in New Zealand is between 3.4 and 8.1 per cent of gross domestic product (GDP), which measures the dollar value of market activity in the economy.[18]

An important feature in Wairoa is the diversity of professional skills that the volunteers bring to their roles. These include leadership, administrative and communication skills, financial and fund-raising experience and computer skills. Their willingness to share these skills offers a clear link between the formal and informal economy, but this extends much further.

Almost all respondents (36 of 39) identified skills they had gained or extended through their voluntary activities. These ranged from technical skills, including IT and communications, through to people skills, including empathy, patience and endurance. In this way, the informal economy acts both as a reserve of skills and a training ground for the formal economy, a role recognised by many organisations. It has a heightened importance in training, given that one-third of the population in Wairoa has no formal educational qualifications and the unemployment rate is 11.7 per cent.

It is paradoxical that despite the scale of the voluntary sector in Wairoa, the town is struggling. There is a shortage of volunteers at almost every level, but in particular a shortage of individuals prepared to take on leadership roles. The existing pool of volunteers is stretched thinly, and the workload is increasing. For example, Rotary Club of Wairoa was recently required to deliver Meals on Wheels every five months rather than every six months, as it had done previously, because another volunteer group had to withdraw from the roster due to the age of its members and its consequent inability to make deliveries. In some voluntary groups, burnout is a significant threat.

Reconciling the facts and building capacity

The most significant change in land use in recent decades has been afforestation. The boom in the 1990s, which was not driven by state involvement, included planting on formerly agricultural land.[19] Farmers had previously planted trees largely for environmental reasons and to protect their land. Consequently, planting was primarily on the most erodible slopes or on sandy areas of least value to pastoral farming.

In the 1990s afforestation was viewed as an alternative land use that would provide an additional income source. Farmers who had planted or were planting trees at that time disclosed in interviews their concern at replacing grass with trees, describing themselves as 'part of the problem'. They believed that the traditional family farm better supported a healthy community structure, that afforestation contributed to the hollowing out of the community, and that in planting trees they were squandering the hard work of their ancestors.

A 1997 report looked at the implications of afforestation, including employment and household income.[20] It concluded that the opportunities for Wairoa depended on the ability of the people to capture them, since forestry in the district was 75 per cent dependent on contract workers from elsewhere. It predicted that without the establishment of a wood-processing plant in the district, employment opportunities and income growth would be severely constrained. It noted the potential implications for roading, biodiversity, water quality and community life. No wood-processing plant was established.

Issues such as roading (including access for felling) are ongoing concerns and overall resistance to afforestation has increased.[21] Hacking away at the bush to get the first grass cover on in its place was described by New Zealand professor of geography George Jobberns as 'the outstanding achievement of our people in the making of the present landscape'.[22] This image retains a powerful hold on rural New Zealand, including Wairoa.

Development and employment in Wairoa remain widely viewed as underpinned by its land base. Despite undoubted challenges, agricultural development continues to occur on many farms alongside entrepreneurial efforts to develop complementary business activities. Investment and development, including training for young Māori, are also occurring on extensive areas of Māori-owned land.

In 2016, despite continued closure of retail outlets, optimism was boosted enormously by the establishment by Rocket Lab (an American aerospace manufacturer with a wholly owned New Zealand subsidiary) of its priority launch pad on Māhia Peninsula. The investment has provided a high-profile basis for Wairoa to become a player in high-tech industries, generating jobs in roading, infrastructure and tourism. Securing this investment is directly attributable to the hard work of the Wairoa District Council and has encouraged a new perspective on Wairoa's physical environment and the potential for a more resilient future that combines physical assets and social capacity.

Implementing resilience

One challenge is whether resilience in all its complexity will remain a conceptual ideal or can be used to address real-world problems and community needs.

The ultimate drivers of change, and the most important component in building a resilient community, are people. Improving their lives and building their capacities is the primary objective. The bottom line is supporting an environment in which they can thrive. As described, rural communities such as Wairoa are resilient only if they are viable places to live as well as make a living. Narrow concepts of economic well-being are not enough.

Although agriculture, forestry and fishing remain the major economic sector in the Wairoa district (employing 22.7 per cent of the population), a central message from the East Coast Hill Country Conference 2015 was that farm systems 'are increasingly challenged by emerging and compounding factors that make these systems more complex and volatile: globalised markets, a changing climate; increased community expectations for stewardship of natural capital; the health, safety and welfare of people; food and animals; and . . . freshwater quality'.[23]

As with any small town or district, Wairoa's resilience hinges on its ability to capture new opportunities. This requires assuring the development and maintenance of institutional and social structures that facilitate cross-community collaboration and deliver knowledge and services for local capacity building. The informal economy can play a key role, as do public festivals, such as the Wairoa A&P Show, that celebrate patterns of life and links to the landscape and affirm identity. However, the contribution that rural places make to the wider regional and national identity and the long-term opportunities they provide also need to be recognised.

Much of the current debate on resilience for small townships and districts across New Zealand centres on managing change and promoting regeneration. Running through the debate, however, is the idea of a coordinated process to address environmental, institutional, economic, cultural and social challenges in places where people live and work; ultimately it concerns people's well-being. The process extends across the field of public policy and draws on multiple and diverse areas of expertise and understanding.

The optimism boosted in part by Rocket Lab has been increased by the government's pledge to invest in the Wairoa district through the Provincial Growth Fund. This includes a commitment to restore and improve rail links to Napier and Gisborne and could extend to roading and tourist facilities. Such national investment highlights the fact that local, district and regional resilience is not solely under local control; funding from central government may be vital for local initiatives.

The issues of scale and power will be tested in the afforestation proposed as part of the Provincial Growth Fund. The negotiations required between different levels of government offer a move away from a sectoral strategy to the place-based policies that are internationally recommended and locally required.

The example of Wairoa shows that both the problems rural communities face and the solutions to secure resilience require broad-based, cross-sectoral, multi-level initiatives that support action at a local level. They require local knowledge and understanding to identify assets and to build local capacity. They require local institutional arrangements that facilitate cross-community collaboration, the sharing of knowledge, and provision of services. They also require a vision that is rooted in a recognition of the special characteristics of rural places and a commitment to the well-being of the people who live in these places.

Chapter 3 —

Talking to communities: How other small towns view their resilience

— Penny Payne

If you've ever driven through rural New Zealand, you'll realise that Wairoa is not the only struggling small town in the country. In this chapter we share insights from four other rural towns — Te Kūiti, Taumarunui, Dannevirke and Huntly — based on community workshops held in each of these towns between February and April 2018. We spoke with around 50 community members across the four towns about local issues: what they were proud of and how they view the resilience of their respective communities.

We aim to shed light on the current state of these communities and explore some of the issues that are important to them, thereby providing local and central government, community members, planners and policy-makers with a more accurate picture of resilience.

What's going on in our rural communities?

To start, we asked the participants to talk about the things they like about their towns and the issues that they see in their communities. They raised many common issues — both benefits and challenges.

The benefits —

Participants noted a host of reasons why they chose to live in small towns and what it was about their towns that made them happy or proud. These reasons typically revolved around social resilience, namely 'whānau and whakapapa' and a 'close-knit community' that was 'friendly'.

In one town the mayor was described as 'well connected to the community'. This friendliness was seen in people greeting each other on the street, knowing each other's names, and having community support. But, more than simply being friendly, these towns had social capital, with a 'strong volunteer mentality', and 'lots of community driven action'.

People saw this social connectedness and supportiveness as a type of 'reserve tank' of resilience: something to draw on when needed. This was captured in the comments that community members would provide 'koha when needed' and had a 'can-do attitude', and that their town 'might be small but has a huge heart'.

These statements also suggest that resilience can be drawn on in different ways: for social support, and for financial and cultural support. They raise the question of how different types of resilience interact — how social resilience works with economic resilience. We'll explore this idea a little further on.

Community members also acknowledged the value of the infrastructure that supported social activities, such as art classes, Citizens' Advice Bureaux, good schools, clubs and community houses.

This infrastructure was described as fundamental to promoting social resilience; it provided places for socialising and opportunities for community members to invest in the community.

The significant volunteer workforce was frequently mentioned as the infrastructure that kept these things going, with 'good people, people [who are] trying to help'. This extended to St John New Zealand, Meals on Wheels, 'violet ladies' (who fund-raise for domestic violence support), Fire and Emergency New Zealand, and even specific areas of infrastructure such as funeral parlours. Such services allow the towns to be more self-sufficient and more connected.

People also mentioned the environment that these towns provided. These comments could be divided into two categories; the first category being the perks of living in a small town — such as living with 'no traffic lights or parking meters', a 'slower pace of life' and 'an intangible quality'. One individual liked that they were 'invisible'. For some residents, this small-town quality extended beyond their town, with one participant describing their community as 'grounded — keeping it real'. Another commented that their town 'has a strong voice in the health sector', while another mentioned that their 'local club reach[es] out to help other clubs build up their numbers'. These comments suggest that some small towns see themselves as providing a unique perspective and show the value that connectivity can bring.

The second category of comments focused on the physical environment. They included the towns being 'close to the river', with a 'beautiful valley, [which is] colourful, especially in autumn'. There were numerous examples of community members' special spots, like the 'river viaduct', 'beautiful lookout', 'railway historical cottage' and 'community gardens'. Several people also described their towns as being 'so very central'; for example, Huntly being 'handy to Hamilton, Auckland, Raglan and Mount Maunganui'. This makes it 'easy to travel', with 'less than an hour to city centres', and adds 'tourism potential'.

The scenery may be beautiful, but it is
becoming increasingly difficult to attract farm
labour to work in rural areas.

Overall, these comments highlight that the social, institutional (e.g. clubs) and environmental aspects of small towns also make them great places to live.

The challenges —

Communities also talked about the issues they saw. Many of these relate to what are intergenerational and interconnected social issues. These include domestic violence, mental health problems, gambling, crime and suicide. People mentioned gang culture, drug use, poverty and homelessness. In one town, the escalation of these issues had resulted in high fences being erected, which was 'starting to make the town look like a concentration camp'. People wanted the town to 'clean up the shops, broken windows and shop rubbish'.

In fact, communities reported that the types of shops and facilities were an issue, with 'too many fast food outlets', 'too many alcohol outlets' and 'a lack of sporting facilities'. This indicates that the local built environment is important to the way people feel about their towns and suggests there is a connection between the built environment and social issues.

Community members also raised issues relating to the local economy and infrastructure, such as a lack of transport despite the proximity to surrounding cities. Inadequate housing (quantity, quality, affordability) and a lack of employment opportunities were also raised.

Participants saw a negative cycle regarding housing, saying there was not enough high-quality housing, which provided a disincentive for wealthier people to move to the area and therefore an ongoing lack of investment in the housing stock. One community member referred to the 1980s, when there was a wealth of government workers in rural New Zealand. These workers bought and maintained the larger, high-quality housing. With the loss of working-age people from the rural regions, people stated that lack of investment in these houses is a real issue. They also discussed the problem of small ratepayer bases being spread over a wide area, which is a characteristic of most rural towns.

The notion of a lack of population to support infrastructure such as housing leads some to the conclusion that attracting or retaining people is the 'silver bullet' solution for these towns. Attracting people could promote job growth and local spending, and alleviate some of the social issues mentioned above. One person expressed the need to 'make it more appealing so people will move here to work and live'.

While this strategy may seem obvious, it is actually very complex.[1] Attracting people can be extremely costly and beyond a community's means. In addition, attracting people does not significantly affect the overall trajectory of a town and can result in a loss of people from surrounding areas. In the case of the communities we spoke to, the solution didn't seem as simple as making sure the population was growing. One woman told of how she retrained outside the region with the intention of bringing her skills back. When she returned, however, there were no jobs that enabled her to contribute to the community, so she had to commute out of town for work.

Others acknowledged this phenomenon, noting problems retaining medical staff; shortages of teachers, doctors and police; and a 'need for good leadership' within the community and local councils. So, despite the call for higher-paid professionals who could fill the higher-end housing stock, a range of related issues could well reduce the effectiveness of attraction strategies. This relationship between retaining skills and maintaining and building infrastructure was raised time and time again in our discussions, and appears to be circular (loss leads to more loss) and complex.

Finally, communities described a lack of understanding from outsiders of their issues, and a lack of local control over decisions. They saw a lack of a national voice with rural insight, 'unforeseen impacts of government policies on our community', and a 'lack of systems thinking' regarding rural communities. One example is the One Billion Trees initiative, which was seen as threatening rural communities through the loss of jobs. Forestry was seen as a 'detrimental policy', because there 'is too much money going out [and] logging [is] putting nothing back'.

These communities see a need for industries that provide longer-term work. The ideas proposed by central government were described as 'one-size-fits-all solutions' and 'dangerous', as community members wanted 'long-term diversity of income' and 'opportunities for young people'.

This feedback highlights the need for a consultative approach towards national and regional policies to ensure that these perspectives are heard. It also highlights the need for more nuance in how they are implemented, acknowledging how they might affect each area respectively and affect rural communities differently from their urban counterparts.

Estimating resilience

The next activity in each community workshop was a quiz. We had gathered statistics from the 2013 and previous New Zealand censuses and other government data sources (e.g. regional council websites) on education levels, unemployment rates and percentage of te reo Māori speakers. We asked the workshop participants to guess how their towns performed on these statistics. The purpose of this activity was to give community members an idea of what the official statistics indicated and to encourage them to think about and discuss these statistics.

There were some interesting patterns in how communities tended to overestimate or underestimate these statistics. First, regarding social resilience, community members were consistently more positive about social aspects of their communities than official statistics suggested. On average, they estimated that volunteering rates were 31 per cent higher than they were, and that 15 per cent more adults had finished high school than official statistics showed. They also estimated population growth as being 10 per cent higher than it actually was.

In discussing and evaluating rural resilience it
is important to ask what resilience means to
different members of rural communities.

This fits with how participants focused on social aspects of their community as their strengths — volunteering, friendliness and community spirit. This gap between perceptions and reality might also be somewhat explained by an observation from one community, that the nature of participation in rural communities was slowly changing; newcomers seemed to be less connected.

This was thought to stem from an increasing busyness: people had to work more because a single income was no longer enough to support a household. People also described less commitment to the community — less willingness to contribute time to volunteering. This phenomenon, they said, was having flow-on effects for the maintenance of social infrastructure, such as schools and sports. The issue was evidently close to participants' hearts, as it was described as a 'lack of loyalty', where 'previously, rural people were more traditional members of the community'. This perceived lack of loyalty does not yet seem to have affected community members' perceptions of key social measures, however.

Turning to cultural resilience, ratings were relatively close to actual statistics, including the percentage of people who spoke te reo Māori, the percentage who identified as Māori and the percentage who were born overseas. Interestingly, however, religious affiliation was underestimated by 10 per cent. Some people thought that the official data was overstated, because it represented people 'ticking a box' on a form rather than actually attending church services. Actual religious participation was seen to be declining in one community.

Interestingly, we found that communities with higher levels of religious affiliation tended to think they had lower cultural resilience. It is hard to explain this tendency, beyond noting that the workshops saw their religious communities as 'not vibrant'.

Results from the quiz across the four communities indicated that economic resilience was both underestimated and overestimated. Median income was estimated to be $9000 more than it is, while unemployment rates were estimated to be 7.7 per cent higher than they are. Thus, although community members overestimated income, they were aware of employment and income issues. Comments about 'not enough opportunity for employment', 'lack of employment' and 'poverty' were common.

Overall, workshop participants had more positive perceptions of their towns than the statistics indicated. This tendency perhaps indicates that community members have a functional optimism bias: they see their town in a good light, which helps them to continue living there and see the benefits rather than the challenges.

Community ratings of resilience

At the end of each workshop, we asked participants to say how resilient their towns were. We asked them to rate the social, economic, cultural, environmental, institutional and overall resilience on a scale of 1 to 10 (10 being the best). Given these insights about the positives and negatives of the communities, and after hearing the correct statistics, how did communities rate their resilience?

Overall, resilience was rated as moderate, at 6 out of 10. Economic resilience was consistently seen as lowest, with an average of 4.3. This result is interesting given that communities overestimated economic statistics, although they also remarked on many economic issues. On the other hand, cultural resilience was highest (6.2). This result may be due to a strong Māori presence in these towns, reflected in comments about 'being part of a Māori community', 'whānau and whakapapa', and a generally multicultural perception of 'all cultures'. For ratings on social, environmental and institutional dimensions, resilience was seen to be moderate (5.8, 5.8 and 5.3, respectively).

What do these numbers mean? It's important to note they do mean something, as the community members making these ratings have spent an average of 31 years in their town.

The original purpose of these workshops was to test how to measure and think about resilience. We also looked at the relationship between official statistics that could be used to benchmark resilience, and how communities rated their own resilience. Overall, we found that some statistics were related to communities' own ratings of resilience, but not many. These included the proximity to the nearest town centre, voter turnout, state-owned houses and self-rated health, which were all related to institutional resilience. Interestingly, phone access and voter turnout were related to social resilience, but in the opposite direction to what was expected: more access meant less social resilience, and more voter turnout was related to a lower perceived level of institutional resilience.

Although some of these findings are curious, it is also worth noting that none of these statistics were significantly related to communities' overall ratings of resilience.

These results suggest that we should be cautious when using statistics to describe rural communities. Statistics should not be used in isolation to describe how a community is doing. Moreover, factors that are thought to be positive, like internet access, may not affect a community in positive ways. We are not, of course, advocating for no internet access for rural towns. We are suggesting, rather, that resilience is complex, and consultation with these communities to see what is happening 'on the ground' is critical.

Can we accurately judge towns as 'more' or 'less' resilient?

We now move on to a different but equally important topic, and the question is this: if we can't use statistics to decide how a community is doing, can we use expert judgment? The media, for example, likes to make judgments about rural towns and how they are doing: are they thriving or dying, winning or 'just surviving'? These blanket statements often appear in popular newspapers or online articles and can seriously affect how a town is perceived by outsiders.

We asked the question, can these types of statement be made with any accuracy? To test this idea, we convened a group of experts who conduct research about New Zealand's rural communities and their resilience. They categorised two of the four towns mentioned in this chapter as 'more resilient', and two as 'less resilient'. The next step was to test whether the categorisations fitted with the communities' own perceptions of their resilience; were the experts accurate in their choices of those towns that were doing well? This test showed that the expert ratings did not match communities' own ratings of resilience. In fact, it was difficult to separate out two towns as 'more' resilient. It was more complicated than this, with different towns having different strengths and weaknesses.

This tells us several things. First, expert judgment alone should not be used to make decisions about rural communities; for example, about government policies. A town might appear to be struggling, and perform poorly on key measures like income, but community members might be doing just fine.

Second, internal and external perceptions of a town differ. Living in a community provides a different perspective from reading about it or visiting it; some superficial judgments might not be correct. Finally, blanket statements about towns 'dying' or 'thriving' might be oversimplifying things; a town's resilience is affected by many different factors.

So, statements from the media about 'the dying small town in rural New Zealand' may not, in fact, be true, and certainly are not helpful for a community. Given that using expert opinions and statistics about resilience has mixed success when describing what is happening on the ground, it is critical that community members themselves have their say.

How does community resilience work?

As we have discussed, community resilience is complex, so it is difficult to find a simple way to talk about, measure and capture it. The next section discusses possible ways of doing this.

Before we get there, the workshops with the community helped us with one more research question: testing how resilience works. We wanted to understand whether it was possible to divide resilience into dimensions, and whether together they make up 'overall' resilience.

We tested this idea by having communities rate each dimension of resilience, and then testing how the dimension ratings related to their overall ratings of resilience. In some towns, some dimensions of resilience related significantly to overall resilience — social for one town, cultural for another, and for one town, none at all. Across all the towns, social, cultural and institutional resilience related significantly to overall resilience levels. This relationship was strongest for social resilience.

This is a good thing, because across the towns, statistics around social resilience were overestimated, and most of what community members were proud of related to social aspects. So the fact that social resilience was most strongly related to overall ratings of resilience perhaps contributes to higher resilience ratings overall (this references the optimism bias discussed earlier).

Last, the research team tested whether together, the resilience dimensions (social, cultural, institutional, environmental and economic) could be collated for a 'total' resilience. They found that, indeed, they could. For all towns, the relationship between the sum of the parts and the overall rating of resilience was strong.

This result tells us that we are probably thinking about resilience in the right way. First, it comprises a group of subcategories or 'types' of resilience. Second, by themselves these types cannot be used to accurately describe resilience — just as statistics about a single part of a community (e.g. the economy) cannot be used to benchmark a town's overall resilience levels.

Finally, these different types of resilience might be somewhat compensatory — more of one dimension can make up for less of another. This might be why it is inaccurate to say that a town is dying just because the population is dwindling. It also makes these towns more adaptable, and therefore more resilient.

So what are the implications of these findings for community resilience? On one hand it tells us that if a community is really struggling on one front, such as the local economy, it doesn't mean the end of the road. If there are healthy levels of other types of resilience, this might be okay for people in the community. On the other hand, the interaction between the different types of resilience makes it more difficult to identify thresholds or tipping points of resilience — how little is too little of one type, and are there certain combinations of types of resilience that support communities facing change?

More work is needed to examine these questions, but it certainly seems that social resilience is a pivotal component of overall community resilience.

Chapter 4 —

The Sustainable Land Use Initiative: A community's response to an adverse event

— *Alec Mackay*

The massive storm that hit New Zealand in February 2004 had the greatest impact on Manawatū and Whanganui. The resulting flood was the first such incident to occur under new civil defence legislation and constituted the largest emergency management event in New Zealand for 20 years.

Central government estimated the total cost of damage in the lower North Island at approximately $355 million, with the total cost of flood-related damage estimated at almost $400 million.[1] Roads in the region sustained damage costing $65 million; four bridges were destroyed and 21 were seriously damaged; up to 2500 people were displaced. One month after the flood, at least 500 homes remained uninhabitable.[2] The flood also caused substantial breaks in road networks and disruption to telecommunications, sewage treatment, and water, electricity and gas supplies.

This chapter examines the impact that this 1 in 100-plus year storm had on the region and describes the resilience of the community at that time and since.

One response from the farming community and the region to the devastation was the Sustainable Land Use Initiative (SLUI, or *slew-ee*). Launched as a direct consequence of the storm, SLUI was designed to:

- reduce erosion rates closer to natural levels;
- build resilience in the rural sector and in the regional economy;
- protect lowland communities from the effects of upstream hill-country erosion; and
- improve water quality in the region's rivers.

This chapter focuses on how the region worked with SLUI to 'bounce back' from the storm, and describes the resilience of the community at that time and since. Bouncing back from adversity — whether it is a single event or long-term trends — is a large part of resilience. The resilience process in this case shows the importance of people and their interactions and provides lessons for everyone in rural communities — farmers, other community members, local government and farm consultants.

The storm's impacts on the region

Horizons Regional Council, the second biggest in the country, covers 2.5 million hectares and includes Manawatū and Whanganui. Sheep and beef farms within a two-hour drive of Feilding produce two-thirds of the lambs for export from New Zealand. Enormous scope remains for lifting the productivity of both the Manawatū Plains and 1.2 million hectares of hill country.

Rural landscapes not only contribute to the economy but also provide a range of other services, many of which people tend to take for granted. They regulate flooding by absorbing rainfall; they filter and provide much of our drinking water. They provide recreational services, and are a place in which to connect with our living environment. Rural New Zealand also contains some of our remaining indigenous, and in some cases endangered, flora and fauna. It is certainly somewhere we take overseas visitors. The closing of the Manawatū Gorge road because of slips and the loss of State Highway 1 in the upper South Island following the Kaikōura earthquake of 2016 highlight the importance of the road networks that pass through rural landscapes.

Our young geological features and physical location make a large part of New Zealand susceptible to extreme storm events, and the massive cyclonic storm that hit New Zealand in February 2004 is one of numerous examples that highlight our vulnerability. The damage sustained in that event was a wake-up call for the Horizons region and the country.

Many rural people were unaware of the impending flooding until it was too late to move important equipment and livestock. More than 2000 farm properties experienced flood damage, with 800 properties seriously affected.[3] Milking sheds, fencing and tracking, irrigation facilities and access roads were either damaged or destroyed.

Inevitably, farm production was adversely affected. In monetary terms, the direct effects included drowned livestock, interruptions to milking and the destruction of crops. Grazing was lost to erosion, and damage to farm tracks and fences resulted in the loss of livestock, feed and pasture control. The flooding and subsequent silting also caused substantial damage to and losses of plant, equipment and buildings.

The cost to dairying was an estimated $41 million; sheep, beef and deer farming $66 million; crops $24 million; and forestry $29 million.[4] In the hill country, 62,000 individual landslides were recorded, covering 18,000 hectares. In total, some 29,000 hectares were severely eroded.

In addition to the direct effects of the flood, Horizons Regional Council identified the loss of soil and productive capacity as reducing regional GDP by $141 million for the 2004–05 June year. Estimated long-term losses included the cost of resources diverted to farm repairs rather than improvements and innovations, stifling growth and limiting the ability to respond to opportunities. Pasture production losses from slip damage are expected to take 30 years just to recoup 50 per cent of pre-erosion levels.

An estimated 200 million tonnes of soil were lost from the region. The large quantities of soil deposited downstream lifted the riverbed and reduced the protection of infrastructure and farmland provided by the existing stopbanks. The erosion and resulting sediment also had significant and ongoing negative effects on water quality.

The storm's impacts on people

Several researchers, including those associated with Resilient Rural Communities, worked to understand the experiences and responses of those affected by the flood. Using a survey and face-to-face interviews with farmers and others associated with the floods and their aftermath, they obtained new insights into community preparedness, responses and resilience in the face of disasters.[5]

The study by Smith and associates made the following observations:

- The resilience of rural communities is shaped by a wide array of economic, social and political drivers that operate in isolation from any debate on resilience or disaster management.
- It is the coherence and strength of communities that underpin the

The Manawatū floods of 2004. Severe weather events such as this challenge the resilience of farms, farmers and their rural communities.

capacity of individual farm households to respond to adverse events.

- The flood forced people to rethink what or, more correctly, who constitutes their community. In certain cases, this revealed a complete breakdown of community. Such a realisation links these individuals to the long-term hollowing out of rural New Zealand where the loss of services is compounded by a lack of young people.
- Farming in New Zealand, for the most part, remains a family enterprise. For farm families, the farm remains both a business and a home. While farms have become bigger, staff numbers beyond the farming family have not increased.
- The emergence of technologies brings with it opportunities and efficiencies, but these are not always matched with increased resilience during an extreme event.
- Farmers themselves, confronting adverse events, often require broader community support. Consequently, building resilience must go further than any narrow focus on the economic productivity of the land.
- There is a growing recognition among farmers that many of their land-use practices need to change if their farms are to become sustainable. However, achieving the goal of sustainability requires more than an appreciation of the importance of appropriate land-use practices among farmers.

The research team concluded that the sustainability and resilience of the community as a social organism must be viewed within a context of ongoing rural decline in which the health of both the individual and the community has suffered.

The response: SLUI

Implementing a 'mountains to sea' approach, SLUI was born out of crisis. Its aims were to protect people and assets from future storms, protect the soil assets upon which our rural economy depends, and reduce the region's reliance on government relief in the future.

It is important to recognise that policies for erosion control in New Zealand are not new. We have a long and incremental history of soil conservation dating back to the establishment of catchment boards in the 1940s. Catastrophic events such as major floods bring people together, thrust policy concerns high on the political agenda and commonly accelerate policy change. The 2004 floods in the Horizons region reflect this experience, in that they brought groups of people together (including the Horizons Regional Council, farmers, community members and scientists) and reprioritised soil conservation on the local and national agenda.

Horizons Regional Council recognised and accepted its responsibility to create solutions to the issues highlighted by the floods. The timing of the hui in September 2004 was critical: late enough that communities had made some recovery, but not so late that the effects of the flooding had faded in people's memories. That meeting galvanised the commitment of rural and urban communities to address this challenge by recognising the impacts of the storm on all communities. Garry Murfitt, who was the chairman of the regional council at the time, was a key individual, able to bring together diverse actors around a common agenda.

The major vehicle for affecting change on farms as part of SLUI was through whole farm plans (WFPs). In New Zealand, farm planning has long been used to support environmental management, including soil conservation.[6] The funding of SLUI included a one-third contribution from all ratepayers in the Horizons region, and one-third of the costs were covered by individual farmers. The last one-third was paid by the New Zealand government through the establishment in 2007 of the Hill Country Erosion Fund (the Central Government Erosion Fund had previously lapsed with the demise of the Ministry of Works).

SLUI was set up as a voluntary scheme, with a focus on six priority

The Saddle Road bridge in Ashhurst was
washed away during the 2004 Manawatū
floods. Destruction of infrastructure, and delays
in restoring it, can have serious and long-term
impacts on resilience.

catchments containing most of the highly erodible land found in the region. Focusing on priority catchments and highly erodible land was important, because research had shown that targeting soil conservation on the 10 per cent of farms with the most erodible land could reduce sediment in rivers by up to 50 per cent. This potential was a powerful tool in convincing stakeholders of the value of prioritising the roll-out of the WFPs.

A recent internal review drew positive conclusions.[7] Through this voluntary approach, in its first 10 years SLUI has achieved 31,175 hectares of environmental works (2800 hectares per year), covering 63 per cent of top-priority and high-priority land in the region. This translates into a 6 per cent reduction in sediment and phosphorus loads and an 11 per cent improvement in the visual clarity of monitored in-river sites. By the end of 2012, 369 WFPs had been developed and implemented, covering 295,818 hectares of hill country containing highly erodible land. By mid-2014 around 500 WFPs had been completed, covering nearly 400,000 hectares of the 1.2 million hectares of hill country in the region. Today more than 700 WFPs across 500,000 hectares are in place, and the area covered by plans is still growing.

Changes down on the farm

Twenty farmers in the lower Rangitīkei and Tiraumea areas — two of the priority catchments — who had signed up to a SLUI WFP between 2006 and 2014 were interviewed in 2015. The aim was to examine their views on the contribution of these plans to the environmental, economic and social sustainability of their farm businesses and their local communities.[8] Twenty farmers who had chosen not to sign up to a SLUI WFP were also interviewed.

All 20 SLUI farmers interviewed agreed that SLUI aligned well with the key elements of successful farms, number one being maintaining consistent economic profits. Following close behind was enhancing the natural environment of their properties by maintaining underlying natural capital stocks and ecological functions; supporting their communities, increasing productivity and reducing debt all trailed behind on the list. These interviewees believed that SLUI had a positive environmental impact and had potential long-term economic benefits for their farms, as well as broad regional and social benefits.

The SLUI farmers and those who chose not to join SLUI share many similar characteristics and values. Most SLUI farmers see their environmental work as a continuation of their work as stewards of the land prior to SLUI. Equally, most of those farmers who have not signed up have long-established policies to extend environmental work on their land. Both groups identify funding and time as the primary barriers to any speeding up or expansion of their environmental efforts.

Funding provided to farmers through SLUI was a major factor in overcoming the time and cost constraints of completing more on-farm environmental work than they would otherwise have done. They also supported the view that the plans can be used as a framework to increase farm productivity and growth — the improvement being conditional on the farmers' willingness to use their plans as a framework for strategic land management. This is often in conjunction with shifts in land-use and livestock policies, and increased diversification.

The actual contribution of WFPs to on-farm economic growth and profitability is difficult to disentangle from other changes in farm management. There was no evidence that the on-farm implementation of SLUI reduced the productivity or profitability of farming. Rather, there was evidence that WFPs could provide a useful framework for improved farm management and growth and could better position their businesses for the future. Non-participating farmers commonly feared that adopting SLUI would constrain their profitability. SLUI farmers found the opposite was true.

Impacts on communities and economies

Regional and local economies have benefited from increased production on local farms. They have also been boosted by the expenditure on environmental works, funded through SLUI and amounting to an average of $7000 per farm. For the 20 farmers who signed up to SLUI WFPs, this amounted to a total of $140,000. Ninety per cent of this was reported by farmers as being spent in their local economy — mainly on material supplies and partly on labour. This expenditure flowed on to the regional economy.

There is evidence that the environmental work increased on-farm economic resilience. Based on the central North Island hill-country and hard hill-country results from the annual Beef + Lamb New Zealand Economic Service Sheep & Beef Farm Survey, those farms were estimated to have a gross revenue of $597 to $869 per hectare, so these actions can be estimated to have improved significantly, by 2012, the sustainability of farms that earned between $177 and $257 million in revenue each year.[9]

Most labour involved was contributed by the farmers themselves. Perhaps most telling, however, is the $72 million that has been spent to date on SLUI. Recalling that the total estimated cost imposed by the 2004 floods was $355 million, the ratio of losses to subsequent spending is 5:1 — higher if the ongoing losses are included. Given the productivity increases achieved and the inflow of investment funds channelled through SLUI, farmers' uncertainty around any increase in the sustainability of their local communities might seem hard to explain. Certainly, respondents saw erosion control and flood prevention initiatives as increasing environmental sustainability well beyond their individual farms.

An important aspect involved in monitoring the benefits of SLUI was the modelling of erosion and sediment loss, which showed the magnitude of SLUI's impact on sediment loading into rivers. If the programme continues at its current pace beyond 2018, a 30 per cent reduction in sediment and phosphorus loads is predicted over the next 25 years, with an average improvement in visual clarity of 29 per cent by 2043. Horizons Regional Council used state-of-the-environment reporting to convey the benefits of SLUI to ratepayers in urban areas, in terms of the reduced costs of flood protection. This information demonstrated the benefits of SLUI for all participants.

The traditional approach for estimating the economic benefit of such an initiative is to estimate the extent to which it is preventing the degradation of land productivity. By looking at pasture production levels in the years following a slip, we can estimate the net present value of production from slipped land and compare it with production from non-eroded land using the average gross revenue for hard hill country. On that basis, the value of production loss that would be avoided through the works to the end of 2012 can be estimated at $1.1 million per year and growing. The loss that would be averted due to the full set of works reducing sediment in the Manawatū River by 2 million tonnes would be $4.9 million per year.

The actions taken as a result of SLUI also reduced the risk to lowland farms and urban properties in the Horizons region of being damaged by extreme flooding. Furthermore, it is likely that additional costs have been averted from less extreme events that are more common than the region-wide event in 2004.

SLUI: A case study in resilience

The social ties to other farmers and the wider community helped farmers get through the initial phase after the 2004 storms and subsequently helped to support the farmers who wanted to make changes. Key to the success of SLUI was the engagement of community from the outset and creating both vision and cooperation to link resilience across the wider region.

There was a strong perception by all the farmers interviewed that SLUI has made a major impact on environmental and economic sustainability in the region. In these respects, farmers broadly agree that they and their communities are now much more resilient to future events on the scale of the storm that hit the region in 2004. As well as helping to achieve environmental priorities, farmers are using their WFPs to provide a framework for growth and change. There is clear potential included in the objectives of these plans to extend their use in this way for evolving both farm and regional needs. Maybe the current trend in New Zealand's economic policies for regional growth that favours a market-led, business-focused approach and downplays social and community considerations needs further thought.

There was more qualified approval from farmers for the support provided by SLUI for social resilience in local communities, recognising that SLUI has limited, if any, impact on thwarting the closure of schools, banks, police and social services that are integral to such resilience.

In summary, SLUI provides important lessons for other communities on ways of creating more economic and environmental resilience and how those dimensions interact with social resilience.

2. Making sense of these facts and experiences

—

Economic resilience relies on the ability to maintain and repair vital infrastructure such as roads. However, it is only one dimension of the resilience framework.

2.

Chapter 5 —

A new framework to measure resilience

— *Penny Payne*

We have now painted a picture of the current state of some of our rural communities and explained why we should discuss resilience. However, discussing resilience leads to a series of thorny questions. How do we define and think about resilience? How do we measure it, and how do we track it over time?

This chapter discusses a resilience framework developed by AgResearch in its Resilient Rural Communities (RRC) programme, and shows how we used this framework and how it contributed to our research. We describe the connection between some general ideas and their application to real-life examples. For that reason, this chapter contains useful information for community members, policy-makers, planners and people in government, as well as academic researchers.

Why create a new framework rather than use an existing one, you ask?

We found that no framework existed that did exactly what we needed — communicated things simply, without excess components or complication, yet included enough theoretical premise to stand up to examination. We expect this framework to be able to explain resilience in its complexity, yet still be flexible enough to serve multiple contexts and topics.

Resilience and community as concepts

Resilience and community are both notoriously difficult concepts to define, capture and measure. In our work, resilience is defined as the ability of communities to cope with the external stressors and disturbances resulting from social, political, economic and environmental changes. This definition captures the ideas of both 'bounce forward' — to a new state, by learning and being adaptable — and 'bounce back' — returning to the previous state after a shock.

The second concept to define is community. Our work tends to see a community as a social system located within a specific geographic area. However, we acknowledge that the boundaries of the social system and the geographic area can be blurred. Farmers and lifestyle block owners will likely live outside a town's boundary but will still be part of its social system. They travel into the town to shop, run errands and socialise, and contribute to and help to maintain the community.

People can also be part of more than one rural community at the same time. They can be members of multiple social systems. They can think of themselves in multiple or nested places — the nearest township, the larger town farther away, and the district or region.

Using these definitions promotes a pragmatic and realistic way of thinking about and studying our rural communities.

It is worth noting that the notion of resilience implies that some sort of shock to the system has occurred. Much of the research about community resilience to date has focused on this shock from natural disasters and, indeed, there is another large body of resilience work that focuses on natural disaster 'sudden shock' resilience. But that's not what the framework we have created is designed to capture: our research has been more about slow-moving change that has developed slowly and unfolds slowly — think rural depopulation, technological changes and policy change impacts.

Why do we need a framework?

Beyond the issues raised so far that warrant further discussion, there are several reasons why having a resilience framework is useful.

First, we need to know what comprises resilience. Let's take the use of statistics. Statistics, such as census data, are often used to measure how a community is doing. The Social Deprivation Index, for example, does exactly this, combining statistics such as unemployment, buying cheap food and asking for help from community organisations as a measure of social deprivation. If we were to do this for resilience, what statistics would we use? This question is important, not least because policy decisions taken at a national or regional level need to be based on evidence. Also, as we found in Chapter 3, statistics don't always provide an accurate measure of how communities perceive themselves. Therefore, it is important to decide what resilience does and doesn't include, and then test whether we have included the right elements.

Second, an important use of a resilience framework involves being able to measure or benchmark it. How much resilience does a community have? Does it have more of one type of resilience than another, and how does this make it different from another community down the road? Once we can benchmark it, we can also track resilience over time. This allows us to see how different types of resilience change and whether we are happy with the balance (for example, the balance between economic resilience and social resilience). This is important when thinking about decision-making at community, local, regional and national levels. A benefit of being able to track changes in resilience over time is that we

Rural resilience is multi-faceted and complex and all aspects of it must be considered when thinking about how to build it into farming communities.

can also measure a community's progress toward its goals. This in turn helps to inform decision-making about 'where to from here' for a specific community.

Third, a resilience framework provides a systematic way of testing whether how we are thinking about resilience is correct. It reminds us to think about all the dimensions of resilience and it reveals how we might be focusing on just a single dimension. It also reminds us of other elements, such as resilience types, levels, thresholds and interactions. A framework can be used to generate new questions and provide structures for answering them. In our research, for example, we often came across the idea of 'tipping points' but couldn't express it as a research hypothesis until we applied the resilience framework. In Chapter 3 we discussed how we tested these things, and the results suggested that we were on the right track in the way we were thinking about it.

The RRC programme's resilience framework

The RRC framework discussed in this chapter builds on prior research by identifying the five main dimensions of resilience — social, cultural, environmental, institutional and economic — as shown in Figure 1. These core dimensions are then surrounded by a sixth dimension: the external. The external includes drivers that affect the community; for example, policy and macro demographic trends, such as an ageing population and changes in milk price. This external dimension doesn't contribute to the make-up of resilience as such, but plays a critical role in terms of explaining the context and the drivers. After all, the resilience of a community is strongly affected by drivers outside the community.

Of course, we are not the first to devise the resilience types included here; these concepts are commonly used to reference the multifunctional and multidimensional nature of social systems such as communities. We believe these six dimensions are most relevant for the New Zealand rural community resilience context. Table 1 displays

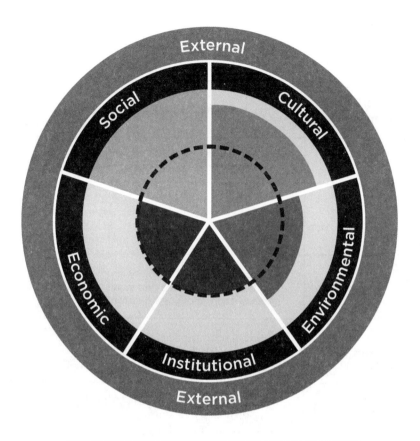

Figure 1. The RRC programme's resilience framework.

Resilience dimension	Elements of resilience
Social	Social inclusion, networks, organisations, health, housing, leisure, education, families, skill base
Cultural	Records of cultural knowledge from history, maintenance of cultural identity, intergenerational practices, cultural manifestations, inclusion in other dimensions of resilience, arts and crafts, tikanga
Economic	Productivity, profitability, employment, infrastructure, debt and equity, industry groups, technology, innovation, value chains
Institutional	Social norms, social licence, regulation, infrastructure, services, social inclusion, local government, Māori institutions, identity
Environmental	Land resources, water, landscape, biodiversity, biosecurity, climate change
External	Natural resource base, national government, international markets, wider society

Table 1. The elements of resilience included under each dimension of resilience in the RRC programme's resilience framework.

a breakdown of the elements we include under each of these resilience dimensions.

The RRC framework incorporates several key ideas about resilience. First, we can quantify or measure it. We can say that there is more or less resilience in a given context (in a community in a certain geographic area). Second, it shows that there are different types of resilience, in the form of resilience dimensions. These dimensions might interact, but they can also be distinguished by characteristics that make them different. For example, employment fits under economic resilience, and housing fits under the social dimension of resilience. However, employment is likely to influence housing, and there are many other interactions between the listed elements of resilience, both within and external to the community system (e.g. education and income, resources and local government, Māori institutions and cultural identity).

The third key idea the framework introduces is that each dimension is considered to be a piece of the 'pie' that makes up overall resilience. There can be more or less of each of the types of resilience, and this influences overall resilience levels. As we found when running workshops with small rural communities in New Zealand (see Chapter 3), these dimensions appear to interact in cumulative and compensatory ways. More of one type of resilience can make up for less of another, so that overall resilience remains the same. This means that, with resilience, an accurate picture of a community might not be obtained if one dimension is extracted and examined in isolation.

Finally, the framework captures the idea that there are resilience thresholds or tipping points, where too little resilience results in a fundamentally different state. In the context of a rural community, this might be a loss of population beyond a sustainable level, and therefore of supporting services, infrastructure, employment and so on. Past a tipping point, the community has fundamentally changed.

Using the framework

Given the theory on which the framework is based, the next question is, how can it be used? The first use of the framework was to examine four case studies in New Zealand.[1] They all involved rural communities but in very different ways. Each of these is discussed briefly here.

Manawatū 2004 flood —

The first case study focused on an attempt to improve the sustainability of land use in the Manawatū-Whanganui Region after serious flooding in 2004 (see Chapter 4). This programme was called the Sustainable Land Use Initiative (SLUI), and it involved farmers mapping their land and working towards reducing erosion; for example, by planting trees. Ten years later, farmers were asked how the initiative affected them. The resilience framework was useful for analysing which types of resilience were affected.

Interestingly, as a result of SLUI, all farmers who signed up to it described an increase in two types of resilience — environmental and economic — on their farms. The increase in these types of resilience at the farm level was also seen as linked to increases of environmental and economic resilience at the regional level. This finding suggests that resilience is linked at different scales, and the right initiative can influence resilience at multiple scales.

As mentioned earlier, however, the different dimensions of resilience can be affected quite differently by the same external stressor and policy response, such as a flood or a land-use improvement initiative. In fact, social resilience was not seen to have increased through this programme and, furthermore, SLUI was not successful in slowing the decline of social resilience. This decline in the years following the flood was evidenced by a reduced population, the closure of services such as schools and banks, and reduced social services.

This is another interesting finding produced by viewing this case study through a resilience lens — that shocks and responses to shocks (such as policy change) can have a positive or negative effect on resilience and may not be strong enough to change some resilience trajectories (e.g. social). By examining a response like SLUI, it is possible to see which parts of resilience are affected by a certain type of response. The benefits of improved environmental and economic resilience would assumedly have a flow-on positive effect for the social aspects of a community, but resilience doesn't appear to be that simple.

Finally, for institutional resilience, which includes regulation, infrastructure and community identity, the flood and resulting SLUI programme seemed to help indirectly. That is, SLUI showed how public policy could increase resilience in the face of community struggles.

For this case study, the framework was useful for describing the effects of an event and the government's response on a community's resilience, and at the level of the farmer and the farm. It provided a useful talking point for the interaction between dimensions — that external responses such as new policy might affect resilience in different or unexpected ways. This leads to a question around the types of resilience to prioritise for a given community, and when resilience might be out of balance. After all, if the community's population declines below sustainable levels, is an environmentally and economically focused initiative the best solution? These are the types of question the framework helps us to consider.

Bicultural biodiversity planning —
The second case study was the Waikato Regional Council's Local Indigenous Biodiversity Strategy (LIBS) pilot, otherwise known as Source to the Sea: Te Puna o Waihou ki Tīkapa te Moana, which examined the benefits of using a bicultural approach to managing biodiversity in the Waihou catchment. This was achieved by creating a 'kaitiaki farm plan', which incorporated Māori knowledge and values combined with parallel Western theory and translated into on-farm practices (see Chapter 13).

Rural events provide an opportunity for town
and country to appreciate the importance of
each group's contribution to agriculture.

This case study is another example of a regional policy to improve environmental outcomes.

This project began with a focus on improving environmental and cultural resilience. It aimed to address the immediate concerns relevant to government, such as land degradation and biodiversity loss. To make the changes sustainable, it was acknowledged that the strategy must also be relevant and integrate Māori values, so a cultural element was included. As the project developed, however, it became clear that Māori values are holistic, spanning across the resilience dimensions. In this context, it was more appropriate to consider the resilience dimensions as highly interconnected rather than separate, because for Māori the preservation of the natural environment is strongly linked to the resilience of the people (social) and all other types of resilience. As such, a biodiversity framework was developed that fitted with this world outlook. The resilience framework is simply a way to describe these differences and bring diverse values together.

Wairoa resilience —

Another case study focused on the work discussed in Chapter 2, on Wairoa and its informal economy. When looking at key statistics, Wairoa appears to be struggling; for example, with employment, population numbers and health. The work in Wairoa looked at the strengths and weaknesses of the community and sought the community's perspective on its future. The framework was again useful for organising the conversation. First, it raised the idea of how to measure resilience. Can this be done by using statistics, such as income and employment levels? In fact, the statistics indicated that things were going badly, but community members perceived their resilience as relatively high. They were proud of their community, supportive of their council, and stable — they weren't planning to move. This is the same finding as that in Chapter 3, from the small towns of Te Kūiti, Taumarunui, Dannevirke and Huntly. In this sense, using the framework while consulting with communities allowed a 'checking of the facts', where the research team could ask the community, 'does this fit with what you know?' in a structured and systematic way.

Evaluating research —

The final example of use of the framework was to assess part of a research programme, the Our Land and Water — Toitū te Whenua, Toiora te Wai National Science Challenge (OLW NSC). The resilience framework was used to structure a review of the research theme called 'Collaborative Capacity'.[2] The framework served essentially as the lens through which to examine the research theme: which resilience dimensions were being considered, and at which scales. This allowed a consideration of where there were gaps, where the focus was, how this fitted with the broader piece of work, and whether any changes were needed.

Briefly, we found that the Collaborative Capacity theme focused on developing organisations and their capabilities, which fits into institutional resilience. The theme focused on stakeholder engagement and collaboration, specifically on creating tools and processes for better collaboration. The interesting consideration here is how this would fit with the broader OLW NSC, which has targets focused on environmental and economic goals. That is, how would an increase in institutional resilience result in greater environmental and economic resilience?

Questioning this required the theme's researchers to be more explicit in their assumptions about how developing capabilities would lead to impacts. The answer was that the theme hoped to increase the number and speed of agreements regarding land- and water-use decisions through building better collaborative relationships. Explaining this helped to create a testable hypothesis for the theme, providing a neutral description of resilience that could be applied to the Challenge.

Using the resilience framework also revealed that different aspects of the programme were working at different scales. The Collaborative Capacity theme tended to work with communities and regions, while the Challenge aims to produce national-level impacts. By using the resilience framework, we could prompt the researchers to explain how they saw the two scales interacting. Consequently, they clarified how achieving goals at a catchment scale (intermediate level) can result in achieving Challenge goals.

A useful framework

In summary, applying the resilience framework to different examples can be useful in many ways, including:

- quantifying amounts of each resilience dimension, for benchmarking and measuring trends;
- looking at the interrelationship between resilience dimensions: how closely they are connected and which dimensions are affected;
- looking at the relationship between the external dimension and internal resilience dimensions: how a policy or outside force affects community resilience;
- considering unintended consequences by keeping all the dimensions of resilience in focus.

This framework can be used across a range of contexts, not just for rural community resilience — although that is the context discussed here. For instance, a school teacher from a small rural town in New Zealand requested a copy of the framework to help geography students discuss resilience. A district councillor also used the framework dimensions to help the council review their 10-year plan. We think it has the potential to serve suburban and urban settings as well, and as a tool for taking a broad approach to well-being in New Zealand.

The resilience framework and the research that relies on it can be found on the Resilient Rural Communities website at www.agresearch. co.nz/resilient-rural-communities.

Chapter 6 —

Creating an integrated perspective with modelling

— Bill Kaye-Blake

Resilience has several dimensions, but trying to get a perspective that integrates them can be difficult. There is a lot to remember, with many interactions happening at once. Computer models are a great tool for creating an integrated perspective. They can be built up piece by piece from bits of information until they are big enough and complex enough for the job. This chapter discusses a computer model that our research team uses to analyse farming practices and regional and national policies, especially for climate change and water issues.

A discussion on computer models isn't for everyone. Nevertheless, it is important to understand the usefulness and limitations of models. As a saying in the modelling community goes, models are to be used but not believed.[1] That is, we need them in order to investigate and analyse, but we should not take their outputs at face value.

The people who will get the most out of this chapter are those with an interest in the link between farm performance and regional or catchment impacts, those who are involved in setting environmental policies for farmers, and anyone who is interested in the rural proofing initiative of the current government.

You already use models, all the time. A 'model' is just a simplified idea of how the world works, and you rely on such simplified ideas a lot. You take facts from the world and select just a few to focus on. Then you decide how the facts lead to some result.

Let's say you want to decide whether to take an umbrella when you leave for work in the morning. You have to make a prediction about whether it will rain. You might look at the weather report and rely on it, or when you walk out of the house, you might look at the sky. You might even consider the season — 'it rains a lot in the spring' — or the recent weather. You take all those facts and run them through your mental model of 'rain'. You just need to know whether to take an umbrella, so you need a model that produces a 'yes' or a 'no'.

Models are always simplifications, but they can be useful nevertheless. The first question is, useful *for what*? In the umbrella model, it is useful to have a model that outputs 'yes' or 'no' when thinking about taking an umbrella. The same model would not tell you the atmospheric pressure at 11.30 a.m. tomorrow.

Because models focus our attention on what we need to know in each case, they concentrate our attention on what is important. We have to decide which facts are in the model and which ones are not. Sometimes, those decisions are made by topic experts. Other times, the decisions are made collaboratively by topic experts working with stakeholders and interested parties. The result might be a different model, but if the job is to develop a collaborative model based on a range of perspectives, then the model is useful for the intended purpose.

Another aspect of computer models is precision. This doesn't mean that models are precisely correct. Precision is about being clear on the inputs, processes and outputs in a model. If we want a model to take something into account, it has to be in the model. We have to tell the computer what the variable is and what data to use for it. We have to describe the processes that convert the inputs into the outputs — you cannot wave your hands around in a model.

Precision is surprisingly important. It is common for people to have a general idea about the mental models they are using and yet be unable to articulate the model precisely until they are forced to specify a computer model.

Models are often built to make a prediction, as in the example of the umbrella. The interesting use of models, however, concerns the what-ifs. What if the predicted probability of rain goes up by 10 per cent? What if it is summer and not spring? A computer model allows us to change the inputs to see how they affect the outputs. It also allows us to change multiple inputs at once: what is the difference between a 30 per cent probability of rain in the spring versus a 50 per cent probability of rain in the summer? By modelling combinations of inputs, we can learn which variables are the most important.

Another use of models is turning the question around. Instead of, 'What is the output from these inputs?', the question becomes, 'If we are concerned about a particular output, what are the inputs that produce it?' A model can help to answer that question.

Our RF-MAS integrated model

Researchers in the Rural Futures and Resilient Rural Communities programmes created and used a model for the work on rural communities.

That model is the Rural Futures Multi-Agent Simulation, or RF-MAS (*arr-eff-mass*) for short. This chapter is about how it works and the various ways we have used it, and how it connects to resilience.

The model has three layers. The first layer describes farmland and its qualities, such as soil type and drainage. The second layer is an inventory of different farming practices. The third, top layer concerns farmers and their behaviour, specifically how they choose their farming practices.

RF-MAS is different from other land-use models in New Zealand in the way it handles farmer behaviour — a point discussed later in this chapter. Information about what is possible on each farm moves up from the land to the farmer, and decisions about what should happen move down from the farmer to the land. Together, the three layers describe the farming in a particular place and how it could change over time.

There are a few things to understand about RF-MAS. The first is that it includes financial and economic information, but it goes much further than that. Sociologists, economists and biophysical scientists have all contributed to the model. The second point about the model is that it includes excellent science from several disciplines. Model data has been published separately in peer-reviewed journal articles,[2] so RF-MAS is based on validated inputs. The third point is that the modelling work is complex: we are trying to understand the linked social-economic-environmental system for agriculture. We use the model to try to get a picture of the catchment or region as a multidimensional system.

The costs of cleaner water

We used RF-MAS to model the costs of cleaner water for the Ministry for the Environment.[3] We modelled 121 farm management options on more than 3000 farms and 1 million hectares. We projected the future farming practices in 25 years without government intervention, and then with 20 different policies. The results can be summarised by focusing on three things: the proportion of land in dairying, the tonnes of nitrogen leached from farms, and the change in regional agricultural production.

We found the amount of nitrogen flowing into waterways in Southland could be reduced. The simplest policies used a blanket limit on nitrogen dressing that applied across all farms. Many of these policies reduced nitrogen losses, some by a little and some by a lot. By creating lower (restrictive) nitrogen limits, it was possible to push farmers to reduce the losses, sometimes by a substantial margin. With higher (looser) limits, policies achieved only a 5 per cent reduction or less.

Some of the highest reductions were achieved by limits that pushed dairy farming out of Southland altogether; they reduced nitrogen losses by 45 per cent. The economic impact of the policies varied a lot. Getting rid of dairying altogether reduced annual agricultural production by over $2 billion. Many policies reduced agricultural output by hundreds of millions of dollars. A few policies were actually net positive for agriculture because they promoted efficiency.

Another important metric is the dollar cost per kilogram of nitrogen mitigated. It indicates the economic costs of the environmental benefit. By itself, it does not measure the size of the environmental benefit or the total economic impact, so it needs to be used alongside other measures. There are several different measures of economic impact. Here, we focus on the value of total production. Total production captures the wider impacts of farms on their surrounding communities and the agricultural contractors, suppliers and labourers. It helps to summarise the impact on rural economic resilience.

Economic impacts varied a lot. Some farming practices made farms more efficient, improving farm profits while reducing nitrogen leaching. Those scenarios are win-wins, albeit ones that require farmers to make changes and perhaps incur some upfront costs. The most restrictive policies reduced production by $440 for each kilogram of nitrogen mitigated. Other policies that used blanket limits across all farmland

The family farm is still the dominant form of farm ownership in New Zealand, but this is changing and these changes have an impact on the vitality and resilience of rural communities.

also cost in the hundreds of dollars per kilogram of nitrogen.

Other policies moved away from blanket limits. Some changed the nitrogen limits depending on the type of soil on a farm. We created policies that gave higher nitrogen limits to well-drained soils and lower limits to poorly drained soils. For the same amount of nitrogen applied to the land, well-drained soils will lose more of it to waterways. To reduce nitrogen losses, farms must reduce the nitrogen applied, which reduces production. When the same limit applies to both the well-drained and poorly drained soils, the economic impact on the well-drained farms is larger.

One variable limit reduced the amount of nitrogen leaching from farms by 13 per cent but reduced total agricultural production by only $60 million across the region. As a result, the loss of production was only $24 per kilogram of nitrogen. This result showed that for lower levels of mitigation, it is possible to make improvements to the environment without large economic costs. It also showed that variable policies were more efficient when measured as dollar cost per kilogram of nitrogen. Efficiency means getting more environmental benefit for less economic cost.

We tried other policies, too. We examined the impact of a 'grandparenting' policy, which allocates nitrogen limits based on what farms had done in the past. Farms that had had high nitrogen use and stocking rates were given higher limits, and farms that had been less intensive were given lower limits. Our scenario allowed current dairy farms to continue, but had the effect of eliminating any more conversions. All dairy farms were also given reduced nitrogen limits to encourage them to mitigate nitrogen leaching. The result was good from a nitrogen perspective: losses were reduced by 25 per cent across the region. However, it was also one of the most expensive policies: annual production in Southland was reduced by $1.5 billion or $320 per kilogram of nitrogen mitigated.

We also modelled mandatory practices to test the mitigation potential across the whole region. The policy required all farmers — dairy and sheep/beef — to use the best mitigation practices. This approach achieved two important results. The first was to get the sheep/beef farms involved in mitigation. These farms tend to leach less nitrogen, but they make up most of the agricultural land in Southland. Achieving small gains over a wide area has a big impact.

This approach did something else as well: it moved farms beyond the minimum activity to achieve a limit to adopting the best mitigation practices available. The policy was therefore process-focused or input-focused rather than output-focused. This combination proved to be a good approach for reducing nitrogen at low economic cost. It reduced nitrogen leaching by 33 per cent at a loss of annual production of only $190 million or $30 per kilogram of nitrogen.

What did these scenarios tell us? The main message is that we have options, but the choices aren't simple. It comes down partly to what society thinks is fair.

It might seem fair to give everybody the same nitrogen limit. That way, we are treating everyone the same. The difficulty is that a blanket limit hits some farms harder than others because of the kind of farming they do or because of the underlying land resource. To avoid uneven impacts, we should perhaps apply variable limits. The flexible policies also have lower economic costs generally for the region because they match the land use to the land resource. That approach means treating farms and farmers differently.

We also have to decide how to vary the policies. If we set the limit according to the type of land, more farmers must make improvements, but some still have higher levels of nitrogen losses. If we set nitrogen limits based on past practices, then we acknowledge the investments made on farms when the rules were different. However, we are also taking away from other farmers the option to intensify in the future. A different way to 'level the playing field' is to mandate specific farm practices. That approach fits the policy to the farm type rather than to land use or historical practices. Mandating practices can impose costs on farmers who are not currently leaching much nitrogen but can produce better economic and environmental results.

Farmer behaviour

The RF-MAS model is different from other land-use models in New Zealand in the way it handles farmer behaviour. It is a multi-agent simulation, a modelling technique that focuses on how people behave. Agricultural multi-agent simulations have been developed overseas. We have had researchers with links to the University of Hohenheim in Stuttgart, Germany, and the University of California, Davis, US, both of which are centres of research on these models.

Multi-agent simulations have two essential features. First, each 'agent' in the model — each farmer in an agricultural model — makes decisions based on behavioural rules. The second feature is that agents interact with each other: they might share information or learn from each other. As a result, social networks matter in multi-agent simulations.

Including farmer behaviours in our model allowed us to test assumptions about them. People have ideas about what drives farmers: lifestyle, custodianship, profit, etc. People also have opinions about different types of farms: corporate farms are more profit-focused, Māori-owned farms focus on the environment, family farms are in it for the long haul. In fact, there is remarkably little evidence regarding the behaviours of different types of farmers. A model like ours allows us to ask the 'what if' question: what if farmers behave in different ways?

We explored this question in work on greenhouse gas emissions. We investigated how farmer behaviour affected the growth of high-intensity dairy farms and found that behaviour did affect the intensity of dairying and thus emissions. The more we assumed that profit drove farmer decisions, the greater the greenhouse gas emissions.

Curiously, because prices and costs vary from year to year, it was not clear that farmers were making any more money. Their earnings bounced around, and sometimes the lower-intensity dairy farms made more profit. We dug into the link between behaviour and profit and found that it is not an either–or problem. When the profitability of sheep/beef was relatively close to that of dairy farming, behavioural rules had a greater impact on land use. When dairying was more profitable by a wider margin, then economic drivers were more important.

We also explored the interaction of mandatory practices and farmer behaviours.[4] In one scenario, some farmers chased profits while others had a more balanced approach. In a second scenario, all farmers tried to make the most profit they could. We put in place a mandatory nitrogen limit and modelled leaching over time.

What we found was interesting. Mandatory policies served as a sort of trigger for action. In farming as in many things, there is a certain amount of inertia: we keep doing what we have been doing. A mandatory policy created a situation in which many farmers had to change; the only question was which change to make. When farmers were focused on profits and forced to change, they converted to dairying at higher rates, leading to greater nitrogen leaching. Their farming practices still complied with the nutrient policies; it was just that the limit seemed to act as a target, as profit-maximising farmers tried to get as close to the target as they could.

What the modelling shows about resilience
The resilience framework is a reminder that resilience has many dimensions that work together. The RF-MAS modelling discussed in this chapter puts some quantitative results on that idea. Because the model has both economic and environmental outputs, as well as a social network of farmers, it shows how much environmental improvement is possible for different levels of costs. We quantified, in dollars and tonnes and percentages, the absolute level of impact, and then compared the options.

The model results also showed that the different dimensions are not in a one-for-one relationship. Depending on the policy, environmental improvements can cost a lot or a little. However, there are also lessons about equity with those policy tools. The total impact on the regional economy, and therefore the community, depends on how policy spreads the responsibility — on who bears the burden. There isn't a right or wrong answer to that problem. Instead, the modelling provides a way to identify who is affected and how. That could be a first step towards crafting solutions.

Most importantly, because resilience is partly about adapting to change, approaches to farming or policy that lock in one set of behaviours could reduce resilience by limiting the ability to adapt. The grandparenting modelling suggests that limiting change makes it costly to get environmental benefits.

The modelling also confirms that people do have options. For example, it showed that dairy farming can continue in Southland even with some limits on nitrogen leaching. Many policies did not affect how widespread dairying was; instead they changed how dairy farms operated. Other policies did limit the number of dairy farms; they tended to remove dairy from parts of the landscape where it has the biggest impacts on waterways. Dairy continued, but where nitrogen leaching could be controlled. These results showed the importance of understanding the natural resource base and the range of options it allows.

The modelling confirmed the importance of considering land at more than one scale at the same time. RF-MAS estimates the economic and environmental performance of each farm and then aggregates them up to the regional level. It is therefore possible to get a sense of both the farm-level and regional impacts of policy.

The importance of this dual perspective is clear with the policy that brought sheep/beef farms into mitigation efforts. Other nitrogen limits tended to affect dairy farms but not sheep/beef farms. From an on-farm perspective, that approach curtailed the leaching from the farms responsible for the highest nitrogen losses. From a regional perspective, however, sheep/beef is a major land use. An approach that both eliminates the highest levels of leaching and produces improvements over large areas can be effective at achieving both economic and environmental resilience.

RF-MAS modelling also confirmed the role of farmers in rural community resilience. We found that how we modelled farmer behaviour affected the results from the model. It affected how farms converted from sheep/beef to dairying and how policies influence conversions and farming practices. The work suggests that farmer decisions are important for the economic viability of rural communities and the environmental impacts of farming. Farmers may be able to play that role more effectively when they have many options for managing farms and when the ongoing processes of demonstration and learning are harnessed.

We know that modelling is just bits and pixels in a computer. We cannot hope to capture the full complexity of rural life in a single model. Nevertheless, RF-MAS has been a great tool for investigating some of the relationships in the resilience framework and in rural communities. It has shown the value of thinking through the implications of policies before they are implemented, an approach the current government is taking in its rural proofing policy. It has also shown that it is possible for rural New Zealand to have both economic prosperity and environmental well-being.

Chapter 7 —

Pathways to future resilience: The TSARA programme

— *Bill Kaye-Blake*

In September 2015 the countries of the United Nations recommitted to making the world a better place. They agreed to Sustainable Development Goals (SDGs) to support equity, sustainability and prosperity. The SDGs fit well with the idea of resilience, and our research team is working to describe pathways towards achieving them.

The work involves an international programme about the role of agriculture in achieving the SDGs. It includes collaboration with policy-makers on how to measure progress towards the goals, and analysis to figure out the land uses and farming practices that fit.

Bringing international commitments into a discussion of local rural resilience might seem odd, but international commitments help to drive national policies, and national concerns set the context for regional policies. These policies in turn affect the choices available to rural communities and farmers. They limit or enable different options at the local level, which affects rural resilience.

The research discussed in this chapter is investigating these connections. The discussion is important because communities are embedded in larger systems, so their resilience is to some degree affected by national and international drivers. As a result, this research is potentially relevant for everyone involved in agriculture and land-use discussions, whether in communities, government or the private sector.

The 17 SDGs describe an ambition for achieving a better world by 2030.[1] They are modelled after the Millennium Goals, an earlier set of goals that were partially reached. They encouraged people to see what could be accomplished with focus and drive, and so the SDGs were created.

The SDGs envision a more prosperous and equitable world and include: No Poverty, Zero Hunger, Gender Equality, Peace and Justice, and Sustainable Cities and Communities. The 17 SDGs are broken down into 169 targets, which provide greater detail. Thus, SDG 1 is 'End poverty in all its forms everywhere', and two targets are to (1.1) have no one living on less than $1.25 per day, and (1.2) halve the proportion of people living in poverty 'according to national definitions'. Significantly for our work, SDG 1 includes resilience language: (1.5) 'By 2030, build the resilience of the poor and those in vulnerable situations.'

The SDGs present a vision that countries can agree to, but they provide little guidance on the thorny details that can cause controversies. For example, the No Poverty goal is to be achieved 'according to national definitions'. Across all the targets, the way in which countries measure progress is left up to them: they get to decide on the indicators.

In 2016 a set of 230 indicators was agreed, but they are simply 'proposed' indicators. Countries are encouraged to create indicators that are right for them. This approach allows countries to tailor their efforts to local conditions, which is important given the different economies, environments and societies in different places. On the other hand, it means that countries have to create the indicators themselves, which reduces the comparability across countries of progress towards targets and goals.

TSARA: Towards Sustainable and Resilient Agriculture

This is where our research comes in. Our team is involved in a programme called Towards Sustainable and Resilient Agriculture, or TSARA for short. TSARA is investigating how countries might meet their commitments to the SDGs in the agricultural sector. It includes Rothamsted Research in the UK, Wageningen University Research (WUR) in the Netherlands, Institut du Développement Durable et des Relations Internationales (IDDRI) in France, and AgResearch in New Zealand.

Each centre is conducting country-specific work and collaborating with the others to learn from the results. The work involves two parts. The first part is connecting with people in policy and agriculture in each country to understand their thinking about SDGs. The aim is to identify good indicators for each country. The second part uses those indicators and a computer model of agricultural land use to explore trade-offs across them. We hope to identify farming practices that are good for both food production and the environment.

TSARA is focused specifically on SDG 2, Zero Hunger, which aims to 'end hunger, achieve food security and improved nutrition and promote sustainable agriculture'. The goal has five targets and our work focuses on Target 2.4, 'implementing sustainable, resilient and productive agriculture', and Target 2.5, 'maintaining genetic diversity in agriculture and related wild species'. The one officially proposed indicator for 2.4 is the proportion of agriculture under productive and sustainable agriculture, while the two proposed indicators for 2.5 are the number of species in conservation facilities (seed banks) and the proportion of local breeds or heirloom varieties at risk of being lost.

Within this SDG, there is a tension. It targets 'productive' agriculture but also 'sustainable' agriculture. It aims to produce enough food at the local level for agricultural communities but also enough internationally for a world of 10 billion people. At the same time, farming practices should ensure sustainability — sufficient resources to allow future generations also to feed themselves. One of those resources is the genetics of the species farmed, including the genetics of its domesticated and wild cousins. Target 2.5 thus seeks to maintain that genetic resource into the future.

The SDGs set a vision for 2030 and 2050. Our research is developing an understanding of the pathways that can get the country from where it is now to achieving that vision. The core method of TSARA is backcasting; we are describing those pathways by working backwards from that future to the present.

The tool for this work is the Rothamsted model, a land-use model that takes into account natural resources and farm practices. For the natural resources base, it uses information on agri-ecological zones, including information about soils, landforms and climate. It then matches those zones with the types of farming that can take place there. For Europe, there is detailed data on the production and finances of farms. In New Zealand, the data is not centralised, but there is still good information on the productivity and finances of different farming practices. Using this data, we are developing a New Zealand version of the Rothamsted model.

One challenge of resilience research is working at multiple scales. At the local scale, the Rothamsted model contains data about farming regions and the types of agriculture in each one. At the international scale, the SDGs are providing the vision for the project and a focus for discussions and modelling. In between, our team is working with national agricultural sectors and policy-makers to describe national indicators, and also working with regional data in the form of agri-ecological zones.

The link across all the scales is the indicators. Internationally, each country will report on the indicators to show whether it has achieved the SDGs, although these indicators are being set at the national level. Locally, TSARA modelling is assessing farm systems in each agri-ecological zone to determine their impacts on indicators; the farming choices will have various implications for soil, water and food production. The model uses the indicators to investigate how farming can change locally to produce the type of impact that each country wants.

Workshops in New Zealand

The TSARA programme includes two processes: workshops with people and modelling of data. The New Zealand research team has held two workshops.

The first workshop, to get views from stakeholders, was held in early 2017 in Wellington. The workshop focused on Targets 2.4 and 2.5 and how New Zealand might go about tracking its progress towards achieving them.

People were invited from many organisations to help identify suitable indicators. There were representatives from central government (MfE, MPI, MFAT and Landcorp), industry bodies (Fonterra, Zespri, Federated Farmers, Business NZ and the New Zealand Forest Owners Association), environmental non-governmental organisations (NGOs) (Ecologic and Forest & Bird) and research organisations (Lincoln University/AERU, AgResearch and GNS Science). In a very New Zealand situation, poor weather kept representatives from Māori organisations from attending the workshop.

The workshop began with an envisioning exercise. Participants described how New Zealand would look in 2030 if the targets were met and how the country would know that they had been met. The next activity was a brainstorming exercise in which participants came up with indicators for the targets. Last, participants collectively identified the most important or useful indicators. After the workshop, our research team reviewed the indicators to see whether they were feasible,

Our research on New Zealand farming through
workshops and data modelling is informing the
global Sustainable Development Goals (SGDs).

depending on whether data was available or could be collected in the future.

A second workshop was held in 2018. Many of the same organisations were represented, with the addition of Te Puni Kōkiri and Stats NZ. The workshop followed much the same process, but we expanded the discussion beyond production and sustainable agriculture to the wider impacts on the economy and the environment. As a result, the discussion included five of the SDGs and seven of their targets.

One key outcome from the workshops and meetings with people across government was learning that New Zealand's SDG indicators had yet to be decided.

Through this process, our team wanted to see how government was going to measure progress towards the SDGs, but by 2018 New Zealand had still to decide how it would show that it was achieving the SDG targets. While there was considerable interest in the SDGs, and workshop participants were keen to bring their expertise to the conversation, the conversation remained at an early stage.

Our research aims to quantify what the future could look like in 10 to 20 years, and then design farming systems and research plans to get there. Agreed indicators are important for doing this work. To help farms and businesses, our team wanted to know how the targets would be evaluated — what government would require from them. To help the science sector, we wanted to establish research priorities: what did government want to know? For our own project, we wanted indicators and data to put into the computer model. We found, instead, that policy-makers were at an early stage in their work.

Our work also reinforced that deciding how to measure progress isn't always easy. For example, workshop attendees came up with several indicators that could be used to measure progress on Target 2.4, 'ensuring a sustainable, resilient, and productive agriculture'. One indicator measured product diversification: the number of different products we produce and export. Data on exports of each product is already reported by Stats NZ, so creating a product diversity index would be straightforward. On the other hand, proposed metrics about environmental health did not seem feasible. One environmental concern is soil health, which can be measured in part by soil organic carbon levels. New Zealand has some scattered data on soil carbon, and creating this index would take considerable work. However, other countries are also interested in and do collect this information. Measuring it might not be easy, but New Zealand may still need to do it.

Modelling New Zealand land uses

This research is also developing the Rothamsted model with New Zealand data. First, we are gathering data on natural resources and farming systems. A database called Land Environments of New Zealand (LENZ) provides an environmental classification of New Zealand based on climate, landforms and soils. The farm systems data is based on several databases as well as industry classifications about the intensity and location of different types of farming.

Next, our team is working with UK researchers to put New Zealand data into the model and has had some success. We began with one farming system, an arable system, which shows what the modelling can do. We looked at options for managing the farms; the options tested were mostly planting dates for the crops, and dates and amounts of nitrogen, phosphorus and manure applications. For each option, we calculated how much each farm produced in crops and what the environmental impacts were. The environmental impacts included the changes to soil organic carbon and how efficiently the farm used the nitrogen inputs. The modelling showed how both production and environmental impacts were affected by the farm management choices.

Modelling showed the trade-off between a better environment and higher farm production and found three key results. First, it clearly demonstrated that there are trade-offs to consider. Maximising farm production has negative consequences for the environment; that result raises the question of how much agricultural production the country wants and how much environmental quality the population wants.

Second, some farm management options were clearly worse for both the economy and the environment. For these options, there are definite win-wins: there can be improvements without giving up anything. Because the model works with detailed farm-level data, our research can even identify the bad management options. Finally, the results also showed that trade-offs are not one-for-one; they are non-linear. The exact trade-offs varied by the specific indicators used, but in some cases giving up a little bit of production can create relatively large environmental gains. However, the more production is reduced, the smaller those environmental gains become.

The modelling suggests that there will be both easy and hard conversations about achieving the SDGs. Some targets focus on food production and others on environmental quality. The easy conversations will be about the win-wins. Our research is showing which combinations of planting dates and fertiliser applications are not particularly effective. With more work, the modelling will be expanded to include livestock and consider other management choices.

The research will identify which combinations of options should be avoided. These are options where New Zealand can improve both the economics and the environment. Once the easy bits are done, New Zealand might find that it is still not on track to achieve the SDGs. At that point, the country might have to deal with harder questions: what do people want the environment to be like, and what will that mean for agricultural production? The harder conversations would be about how to make these decisions and who pays the costs.

A good understanding of community resilience will be important at this point. New Zealanders will need to understand how these decisions affect rural communities if they ask the rural sector to make changes for the sake of the planet.

Taking stock

It has been quite a process so far.[2] Our research has included many people concerned with agriculture — policy-makers, environmental groups, and farmer and Māori representatives. Workshops have revealed the complexity of creating visions of the future. The aims or the goals are easy to state; getting down to measurable, meaningful indicators is harder. Nonetheless, the modelling shows that the effort is worthwhile. There are gains to be had: there are farm management options that are worse than others, no matter how you measure them. There are also trade-offs to understand.

The modelling can demonstrate how much change can be created, and what might have to stop. To have the harder conversations about production and the environment, it will help to have this type of information. That way, the country can base the conversations on specific costs and benefits rather than opinion and guesswork.

This work is still in progress. It has produced a stocktake of government thinking around the SDGs and agriculture, but that thinking is evolving. The modelling has started, but our team wants to add more farm systems and more indicators. Once there is more clarity on the SDGs and more information about possible options, our research can do more to describe pathways to achieving them.

The work has already had some effects. Our early work trying to pin down the indicators led to coordinated work across several of the National Science Challenges. They are creating better links between the science in the Challenges and the needs of government policy. Our team has also talked with a wide range of people to get many perspectives on SDGs, in particular on the interaction between farming and the environment. We have been able to take our new understanding into government, to provide it with evidence about these topics.

It may not sound like much, but we are continuing to give seminars and presentations and participate in working groups, letting people know that there is careful science going on. We think we have an important place in these discussions: we are well informed, concerned with practical farming decisions, and connected to people and communities throughout New Zealand.

The TSARA research has some lessons for work on resilience. The first lesson is about the way the different scales work together. Resilience is both local and not local, which is clear in the TSARA work. The modelling is quite detailed: we researchers are examining how farms in a specific region can apply different levels of fertiliser and manure and what dates they can sow their crops, all on a day-by-day basis.

The first level of decision-making and impacts is at the farm level. However, the whole modelling effort is focused on the big international SDGs; together they are the international vision that provides the drivers for the whole project. In between, our project is managing national-level workshops about the right indicators to develop, and these are helping to create the metrics that will be applied regionally and at the farm level.

For example, SDG 2 envisions a resilient agriculture. That is the big international vision. That resilient agriculture will be measured, however, at the farm level by nationally agreed metrics. The resilience of farms and communities will play out based on what the country decides to measure and tries to achieve; it will be determined both locally and not locally.

In resilience framework terms, the SDGs are external drivers for a local community. They could be positive or negative: they might create pressure and resources to change a negative situation, or they might end up interfering in perfectly adequate local systems. On the other hand, the SDGs are also a reminder that resilience is not solely a local phenomenon. Communities are embedded in many larger systems — all the way up to international systems. There are things that a community can do itself, but also limits to what it can do given the larger systems.[3]

Working with the SDGs is complex and one of the reasons for this is the subject matter. Looking just at SDG 2, its breadth — sustainable, resilient, productive agriculture — is enormous. As researchers, we try to break it down into smaller pieces and we end up with some difficult questions. For example, we have to figure out what 'resilient' means for agriculture. Next, we have to decide which aspects of agriculture we want to ensure are resilient — the soil, air, water, people, families, cultures, animals, crops, genetics, ecosystems, etc. We then have to consider how to monitor and evaluate those aspects to understand whether agriculture is becoming more or less resilient.

There is a lot of information to bring together and assumptions and value judgments to consider. Also, as the modelling shows, even once the indicators are agreed, they are likely to have complex relationships. This raises the second reason the work is complex: it needs many people with different knowledge and experiences to work together. As a result, the process is long and requires effort and commitment. We held two morning-long workshops involving 50 to 60 people and spent days on research and reporting just in trying to agree on a few indicators for a few targets. Because of the complexity of the material and the process, work is still ongoing to understand the SDGs and New Zealand's approach to achieving them.

Research on the SDGs is a microcosm of resilience work. There are noble and worthwhile aims, broadly proclaimed. As a country, we can find easy agreement on these aims, such as ending poverty and hunger. It gets harder when we have to define what we mean by 'poverty' or 'hunger'. It gets harder still when we seek commitment from a broad range of people on definite and measurable steps. That takes time and resources and, ironically, a bit of resilience.

3. How will intersecting drivers affect the future of rural communities?

___

Dairy hub, Southland. Diversification and new land-use options can build resilience into farming systems, but they can also impact on other drivers of resilience such as natural resource management and population demographics.

3.

Chapter 8 —

The resilience of Māori land use

— *John Rendel, Bonny Hatami and Kirsty Hammond*

Ko Tawhirirangi te maunga
Ko Mōhaka te awa
Ko Te Kahu-o-te-Rangi te tangata
Ko Ngāti Pāhauwera te iwi

Tawhirirangi is the mountain
Mōhaka is the river
Te Kahu-o-te-Rangi is the chief
Ngāti Pāhauwera are the people

I n this chapter we take a journey with Ngāti Pāhauwera to paint a picture of what resilience means to them. They have diverse objectives across the resilience dimensions and this chapter discusses research that aims to achieve these objectives.

We believe that a greater understanding of the resources available for production agriculture, combined with the values and knowledge of Ngāti Pāhauwera, will lead to a resilient iwi that is positioned to meet current and future aspirations. We also believe that the balance of Ngāti Pāhauwera landholdings (i.e. plantation forestry and co-managed Department of Conservation [DOC] estate) contributes to environmental, social and cultural resilience, although we have not included this specifically in our research.

First, however, we need to understand where Ngāti Pāhauwera have come from as a people, where they are right now and where they are going. This research step is often overlooked, but it is a critical aspect of our journey.

Tāhuhu kōrero (the back story)

Māori freehold land consists of approximately 1.5 million hectares (5 per cent of the total area of New Zealand)[1] as defined in Te Ture Whenua Maori Act 1993 (the Maori Land Act 1993). This does not include land that has been purchased as a result of te Tiriti o Waitangi (Treaty of Waitangi) settlements or other purchases by Māori entities (e.g. whānau and hapū).

Most Māori freehold land is in small blocks ranging in size from 0.01 hectares to more than 500 hectares, with the average title consisting of 60 hectares. There are many individual owners, from zero to more than 400 people, with the average number of owners per title being 70. This is colloquially referred to as having rights to a 'teaspoon of soil' and, although rarely providing meaningful incomes to owners, does maintain connections to their traditional lands.

Some of these titles will have the same owners and be neighbouring, but the majority are separated by distance and ownership. While these holdings can be fragmented on paper, over time, with whenua (land) purchases and perhaps the formation of management structures across the blocks, they can be managed as larger blocks or series of blocks.

The Ngāti Pāhauwera confederation of more
than 80 hapū is centred around the Mōhaka
River, shown here running through typical
North Island hill country.

The Māori economy is currently worth around $50 billion and growing, and there is the potential for those blocks with a number of owners to become more profitable if management structures were established. However, the cultural, environmental, social and economic (CESE) values of the landowners need to be respected and maintained, which was not the case during colonisation.

Prior to colonisation and land confiscation, Māori managed their whenua in resilient and highly sustainable ways. This resilience can be seen in Māori concepts such as 'kaitiakitanga' (caretaking or guardianship), 'ahi kā' (utilising and defending your whenua, thereby keeping the home fires burning), and 'rāhui' (a closed season or ban, ensuring that the land or waterways were not exploited and were able to regenerate). All these concepts continue to be practised today.

Given the fragmented nature of the ownership of land, however, is it possible for Māori entities to manage with a view to being resilient for the benefit of both current and future generations? And if so, what could this management look like?

Te haerenga (the journey)

Ngāti Pāhauwera is a confederation of 80-plus hapū located in northern Hawke's Bay centred around the Mōhaka River. Traditional communities are Mōhaka, Waihua, Putere, Kotemāori and Raupunga. Pāhauwera (pāhau, meaning 'beard', and wera, 'burnt') comes from a story of a common ancestor, Te Wainohu, who was renamed Te Kahu-o-te-Rangi: they say his beard was burnt when his head was being cured over the fire. Based on whakapapa and settlement in the area, Pāhauwera occupation in the region goes back between 500 and 600 years to the 1500s.

While Ngāti Pāhauwera has in the past been divided into a number of hapū and whānau, each with slightly different rights and each with its distinct territory, the following whakataukī (proverb) sums up the special features of tribal identity that they all share. As members of Ngāti

Pāhauwera, their mountain is Tawhirirangi, their ancestor is Te Kahu-o-te-Rangi, and their river is the Mōhaka.[2]

Their boundaries, or the 'resource area' of their ancestor Te Kahu-o-te-Rangi, extends from the sea at Pukekaraka to Puketitoi to the Waiau River. It is here that he met Te Kapua, a chief from Te Urewera, who said, 'This is as far as you go' ('this is our boundary'). Te Kahu-o-te-Rangi took up his axe and began to make his mark on the bark of the tawai (beech) trees and up on to Te Hāroto, then down into Puketitiri and through the Te Wai o Hingaanga stream to the sea. There was a rock there, a taniwha (water monster), whose name was Moremore, and it belonged to the chiefs from Heretaunga, Tareha, Karaitiana, Tōmoana and elsewhere. From the sea to the east, the boundary then continued until it met again at Pukekaraka. Out in the sea was a demon rock; its name was Tangitu, it was a fishing ground. From there he looked shoreward to Maungaharuru, a mountain that abounded with pigeons.[3]

This narrative helps to explain how the Ngāti Pāhauwera identity is inherently intertwined with responsibilities of kaitiakitanga and their whakapapa connections. R. Joe, in a cultural impact report for a hydro dam on the Mōhaka River, said,

> Our cultural heritage was passed down from
> te Atua [God] to our ancestors and down to us
> through kaumātua and kuia and is called 'ngā
> taonga tuku whakarere iho'. These gifts from te
> Atua include te mana o te whenua and te mana o te
> moana [authority over and responsibility to the land,
> sea and lakes].[4]

This long history speaks not only to the cultural resilience of Ngāti Pāhauwera, but also to the resilience of all dimensions, which are seen as highly interconnected in te ao Māori.

Nōnāianei (where are we today)?

As a result of colonisation — through exchanges where land sales were undervalued, excessive costs were added or promised benefits were not delivered, as well as land confiscations — Ngāti Pāhauwera lost 94 per cent of its land between 1851 and the late 1930s. This left Ngāti Pāhauwera with 5400 hectares of largely fragmented landholdings that had many owners — some without legal access — and rising rates, which prevented the iwi from making full use of its land.[5]

This led to a loss of people from the area over the course of the twentieth century because of a lack of opportunities. Currently, of approximately 7000 registered iwi members, only 1000 are living in the district. This means that cultural identity and values have not been transferred to subsequent generations, which has eroded cultural resilience. This loss of people has also eroded the economic resilience of the iwi, with fewer of its people contributing to the welfare and development of Ngāti Pāhauwera people and rohe (territories).

The loss of land also contributed to a loss in environmental resilience due to land degradation, and a loss of species that are of importance to Ngāti Pāhauwera. As described earlier, Maungaharuru used to abound with pigeons; this is an example of the loss of species on the ranges, such as tītī (muttonbird) and kākā (parrot), which until recently had been completely lost to the area. This loss, in turn, has further contributed to the loss of cultural resilience because knowledge of the uses of and rituals associated with these species has not been passed on to subsequent generations.

In the early 2010s Ngāti Pāhauwera fought back and sought a Treaty of Waitangi Tribunal Settlement because of concerns about 'the long-standing issues in relation to their lands and waters' and the socio-economic consequences of land loss resulting in severe deprivation and cultural disconnection.[6] 'Our ancestors discovered the mana. They found the mana in the hills, in the rivers, and that is why we battle for their return.'[7]

In an effort to redress the wrongs of the past, the New Zealand government, through the Waitangi Tribunal, made a settlement to Ngāti Pāhauwera in 2012 of approximately $70 million, which included 15,000 hectares of forest land, 3500 hectares of co-managed ex-DOC land, and various other commercial redress properties.

Ngāti Pāhauwera Development Trust (NPDT) was the entity that received the Treaty settlement, part of which was Rawhiti Station, a breeding and finishing property (both sheep and beef cattle are bred on the farm and a large proportion of the progeny are sold for processing). The NPDT has since purchased four other farms in its traditional rohe: Pihanui Station (a breeding farm where progeny are sold to other farms to grow for processing); Omahara Farm and Chimney Creek (both of which were purchased as farms that require development); and Kākāriki Station (a farm that purchases young animals to grow and sell for processing).

This initial portfolio of farms was influenced by funds available. The intent of purchasing the farms was to bring their traditional lands back into Ngāti Pāhauwera ownership and create positive opportunities for whānau, the community and the region. Ngāti Pāhauwera Commercial Development (NPCD) manages the commercial assets of the NPDT, including the existing 3500 hectares of farmland.

Te whakahou o te aumangea (rebuilding resilience)

The landholdings of forestry, conservation areas and pastoral land contribute to the rebuilding of resilience for the Ngāti Pāhauwera people. 'Rebuilding' resilience fits with the 'bouncing forward' definition of resilience described in this book (see Chapter 5) — 'bouncing forward' to a new state, as it is not possible for Ngāti Pāhauwera to return to the state they were in prior to colonisation. Given this, how does Ngāti Pāhauwera go about building resilience? Do people work to build resilience to withstand the shock of expected or unexpected future events (absorptive), or do they build resilience to adapt to shocks (transformative)? How does

Ngāti Pāhauwera build this future as they move into acquiring more of their original landholdings?

The potential strategy is long term and connects across the resilience dimensions. First, the return and identification of wāhi tapu (sacred areas) and sites of significance is helping to rebuild cultural resilience. Second, reclamation of land means that Ngāti Pāhauwera members can manage their land resources in a sustainable way, respecting their ancestors and providing for future generations. Third, Ngāti Pāhauwera is working on the provision of areas that can be used for recreational purposes (hunting, fishing, etc.) to enhance social resilience. Last, the regained forestry and agricultural land contributes to economic resilience, as it provides not only employment but also a source of funds that can be used to acquire more land in the rohe.

The long-term objective for Ngāti Pāhauwera — part of their 100-year strategic plan — is to own all their original land again. In the short term, the five-year goal is to have 20 per cent of their landholdings in land that can support horticulture. This may mean land sales or new purchases to acquire the land needed; it will also provide opportunities for whānau land blocks to be part of the horticultural shift in land use.

Understanding the story of Ngāti Pāhauwera reinforces the idea that resilience 'is not an end in itself, but a means to limit vulnerability and promote sustainability'.[8] Sustainability, on the other hand, is more of a static concept, built around different types of capital over which owners have some control (e.g. cultural, natural, social and manufactured).

We can see that Ngāti Pāhauwera is building resilience using a sustainable systems approach. It is interesting to note that resilience and sustainability are very tightly linked: unsustainable practices will magnify the impact of environmental and other types of shocks.[9] These shocks occur in the external dimensions of resilience, such as climatic fluctuations caused by climate change. The shocks have flow-on effects in the system, such as flooding, winds, etc., which are rare events that can have severe impacts.

Given all this, if a farm is to be resilient, it must be sustainable over time, and not only from an economic perspective but also from environmental, social and cultural perspectives, especially for Ngāti Pāhauwera. The history of colonisation, land loss and migration has meant that the Ngāti Pāhauwera people are skilled at adapting to change and creating learning opportunities that have ensured their survival.

Ngāti Pāhauwera is continuing to build relationships within the region and with research institutes and government agencies, both to increase its resilience and to achieve mutual aims. This includes working with Hawke's Bay Regional Council and others on climate change preparedness and East Coast hill-country-specific issues, such as erosion.

In 2015 Ngāti Pāhauwera members engaged with MPI (Ministry for Primary Industries) to begin to explore options. As a result of personnel moving to AgResearch, they became aware of additional capabilities that would help them move through the Resilient Rural Communities programme. Their objectives focused not only on the agricultural production of current whenua, but also on increased pasture and animal performance and, more specifically, what type of land should be acquired next to fit in with the existing portfolio.

An analysis undertaken in conjunction with Ngāti Pāhauwera farm staff and NPDT, using an emerging piece of software called AgInform,[10] helped show how the current farms could operate within cultural and environmental boundaries.

Farms' economic resilience centres on their ability to bounce back to environmentally sustainable positions after adverse events (e.g. floods, major price fluctuations, etc.) and ensure that there are sufficient funds to meet the agreed requirements of both NPCD and NPDT. It also involves the guaranteed protection of areas that are of significance and wāhi tapu.

Before we examine this picture, it is important to note that areas of known cultural significance and existing native bush and areas that were unsuitable for pastoral agriculture were fenced to exclude farm animals (there was also an active pest eradication programme in operation). Therefore, our focus was on the land used solely for agriculture. We saw, over time, how the farms could be integrated through animal and supplementary feed transfers, as well as how individual farms could operate within the environmental boundaries (environmental sustainability and resilience), to maximise the return on money invested (livestock only, as land is not sold but is retained for future generations) and thus contribute to economic resilience.

Predictive analysis has suggested that, as at 1 July 2018, the development will result in a 33 per cent increase in annual profit and a 44 per cent increase in animals (measured as stock units,* not physical animals). There was little change in the variability of annual profit over the planning horizon (10 years). This is important, as increased profitability can lead to an associated increase in variation over time, which can mean a less resilient farming operation. Ngāti Pāhauwera will want to maximise the sustainable profit; however, because both NPCD and NPDT have financial obligations to activities outside farming, we need to be mindful that increased variation may not be sustainable.

Another area of interest to Ngāti Pāhauwera was to ascertain what type of land should be purchased next: should it have physical characteristics similar to Pihanui (breeding property) or Kākāriki (a finishing property) or Omahara (a development property)? Clearly it had to fit in with the current landholding portfolio and add to the economic performance of the portfolio while meeting social, environmental and cultural requirements.

A fixed amount of capital was assumed and the cost and area of each type of land were estimated. Each new farm was added into the analysis in order to estimate its contribution to the portfolio.

---

* One stock unit is the annual amount of feed a 55-kilogram ewe would require to rear a single lamb until weaning (550 kilograms of dry matter).

The best option economically was to purchase another 540 hectares of land similar to Pihanui, as this increased annual profits by 30 per cent. This was surprising because it was the steepest land of the portfolio. The next best was a low-pasture production farm (Omahara physical characteristics), which increased annual profits by 21 per cent, with the least favourable being the purchase of a property with good physical characteristics (Kākāriki-type farm), with an expected annual gain of 16 per cent. This reflected the interaction that exists between land prices (it drives land area that can be purchased), the production characteristics of that land type and the existing land portfolio.

An additional benefit of purchasing a Pihanui-type farm is that the stock policies remain very similar to the current policies; there are simply more animals. All the analyses were undertaken on the basis of expected fluctuations in pasture performance both within and across years.

The analyses provided Ngāti Pāhauwera with additional confidence in its decision-making. This confidence contributes to economic, social and environmental resilience as Ngāti Pāhauwera now has a picture of the farm configurations that are appropriate for its resources, for the present and for the future. It also has a picture of the impact that variation across years has on the farming system and hence the profitability, which enables appropriate decisions to be made when considering the farm livestock policy.

Whakarāpopoto (summary)

We have taken a brief journey with Ngāti Pāhauwera, from pre-European days to the current times, to understand their history, why they are in their current position, and where they want to go to from here. This is an important first step as it helps to inform drivers of resilience and sustainability.

We have been able to use this information to help model farm configurations that are sustainable and resilient to expected fluctuations in pasture and forage growth brought about by climatic variation. These apply to both current and anticipated levels of animal and pasture performance. Furthermore, we have painted a picture that indicates what the next land acquisition could look like. We have been able to do this because we have the appropriate tools and knowledge.

So what did Ngāti Pāhauwera members get out of this journey? They gained validation on previous thinking and some new ideas about how they may use their agricultural land in a sustainable way, thereby building their resilience. This gives them additional confidence in their decision-making, now and for the future.

Chapter 9 —

Southland: An adapting landscape

— Ronaldo Vibart, Vicki Burggraaf and Robyn Dynes

This chapter provides an assessment of Southland as a rapidly changing rural region, as explored in the Rural Futures research programme. It describes the use of workshops where local community members and other stakeholders looked at the key drivers of regional development, potential future land use and the implications of farming within environmental limits.

In this chapter we show the value of models for predicting the impacts of future scenarios on economics and the environment at a regional level. We analysed, for example, increased land area under dairying, nutrient loss regulations, and the removal of palm kernel expeller (PKE) from dairying.

This chapter is therefore relevant to a wide audience, including landholders, those from the primary industry sector, regional and territorial authorities, and anyone interested in regional development or participatory processes.

Participatory workshops

To kick off the idea of identifying and exploring some of the key issues that shape and shake regional sustainable development, four workshops were held in Southland. These used participatory and collective learning approaches that engaged with a range of stakeholders to explore the potential shape of rural regions. Southland was identified as one of two pilot regions, along with Hawke's Bay. These regions were selected because they offer contrasting regional economic drivers and pressures.

The workshops were held with landholders, sector and local government representatives and community members between March 2012 and April 2013. Venture Southland helped to bring together workshop participants with a wide variety of skills and knowledge. The goal of the workshops was, first, to have locals with different backgrounds come together and generate group strategic thinking. Second, for the participants to develop an appreciation of each other's visions and gain a collective understanding of the multiple drivers of sustainable agriculture. Third, to identify actions to take towards a new shared vision. Last, we wanted to create an environment for ongoing interaction and discussion.

A look at Southland

Before we review the findings from the workshops, let's provide some Southland context and a look at how the region has changed in the past few decades.

Southland is New Zealand's southernmost region. As of June 2017, it was home to 98,300 people: just over 2 per cent of the national population. Southland covers an area of almost 1.7 million hectares, of which about two-thirds are in pastoral farming. The region has a long tradition of pastoral sheep farming; this activity dominated its rural landscape during the twentieth century, reaching a peak of more than nine million sheep in 1984. Sheep farming remains the dominant activity in Southland, particularly in hill country, but lowland sheep farms with reliable summer rainfall are gradually being converted to dairy farms. Dairy farming now makes up about 20 per cent of Southland's agricultural land and has been projected to increase to almost 30 per cent by 2035. Dairy cow numbers have increased from 200,000 in 2000/01 to more than 560,000 in 2016/17. These are spread across almost 1000 dairy farms in the region, which was home to 12 per cent of the national milking herd in 2016/17.[1]

The increasing focus on environmental impacts of land use are affecting current and future farming practices. Given the large proportion of land in pastoral farming, the link between pastoral intensification and declining water quality is being increasingly recognised. Although pastoral farming systems are perceived to have fewer environmental impacts, sustained rises in production from increased inputs tend to cause increased nutrient losses and pollutants to air and water. The load of nitrogen excreted by livestock to land provides for a good indicator of land-use pressure at broad scales. Although nitrogen excreted by animals does not necessarily end up in waterways, and some of the nitrogen in waterways will not necessarily have an impact on water use, intuitively it would be expected that the intensity of land use for pasture would affect river water quality. Southland is no exception to this process.[2]

The region also faces population challenges. Concerns about an ageing population are particularly relevant in Southland, compared with the remainder of the country. Projections from Stats NZ show that the average age in the region will shift from 40 to 45 years by 2043. Southland struggles with retaining young people and with attracting professionals and their families into the region from other parts of the country. It does not stop there, however, as the number of people aged 65 years and older

A typical Southland farming scene, but
over the past 20 years the landscape has
experienced many changes.

is expected to increase from 16 per cent in 2016 to 26 per cent by 2043.

There is also the spectre of depopulation. A 2013 report projected that the region's population will decline over the next 20 years to about 88,000, despite a significant number of dairy workers immigrating to Southland each year. In the next two decades it projected that Southland would lose more people than it would gain, and this net migration pattern will make the ageing problem worse.[3] More recent projections from Stats NZ are more favourable, however, suggesting that the population will remain largely stable.

This population concern has not gone unnoticed. Business and community leaders throughout Southland are coming together in an attempt to reverse the demographic trends and attract more people into the region. Several initiatives are being undertaken to grow Southland's population to respond to the workforce shortage; for example, Venture Southland is working with the Southland Regional Development Strategy goal of attracting 10,000 more people to the region by 2025.

About 70 per cent of people in Southland live in urban areas, with 56 per cent in the city of Invercargill. Southland is less urbanised than the New Zealand average, which suggests a lively rural economy and reflects the vital local importance of agriculture and primary industries.

New Zealand has increasingly sophisticated food and fibre industries. They remain the driving force of economic growth and exports, and Southland is no exception to this. Natural resources are a key driver of Southland's economy, with the main industries in the region contributing to national GDP being in the primary sector, manufacturing and mining. The primary sector employed about one-third (more than 17,000 employees) of Southland's labour force in 2012. Red meat and wool (about 8000), dairy (4000) and support services (3000) were the greatest employers, although this is changing. There are more sheep and beef farm conversions to dairy, with many of the livestock and cropping jobs also switching to the dairy sector. Job growth in the region is mostly expected from dairy, support services and the arable sector; this trend will require more engineering trades, support and sales workers, freight drivers and plant operators, but fewer textile and meat workers and sheep and beef farmers.[4]

From interviews with farmers and farm consultants involved in the process, it appears that Southland farm conversions to dairy have stimulated an economic revival and a reversal of population loss. Investments made in converting farms to dairy tend to offset the belt-tightening in sheep farming. The economic development has led to new ways of doing business and restructuring regional networks while reviving local businesses. As indicated by a local farm consultant, the challenge lay in 'creating the infrastructure to actually make the [dairy] industry work'.[5] Some of the social and economic benefits of the land-use change that has occurred have been reported, but less is known about the wider regional sustainability implications.

Community perspective

So, given the evidence that Southland's agriculture is changing, what were the views of the workshop participants? People talked about different aspects of sustainability, the use of limited natural resources, and the dynamics of management adoption and networking within the community. Unintended consequences of actions and policies became vital features emphasised during the workshops.[6]

In addition to a concern over the labour shortage caused by an ageing population base, there were concerns such as the loss of a Southland identity by changing demographics; dairy conversion being perceived as the only option for development; additional pressure on infrastructure; and declining water quality and quantity.

Over the course of the four workshops, community members identified critical factors shaping the future of the region (Table 1). These critical factors have constraints (e.g. having to farm within nitrogen leaching loss limits) and pressures (e.g. dealing with a growing workforce needed by the dairy sector) and communities must adapt and remain sustainable in response to these. The discussions concerned both aspects of resilience: the ability to retain a 'Southland identity' (bouncing back), as well as having the resources to support economic growth (bouncing forward). The workshops aimed to address the following questions:

- Workshop 1: Can we identify and gain a better understanding of the critical factors shaping future regional development?
- Workshop 2: Can we explore current and potential land use 25 years into the future and its immediate and wider implications?
- Workshop 3: Can we come up with three future scenarios and provide a detailed analysis of these scenarios, including information sources and data quality?
- Workshop 4: What were the main findings from the collaborative process and modelling dynamics and outcomes?

Working together, the workshop participants created a few scenarios for the region that could contribute to sustainable regional development. The research team investigated the potential impacts of the scenarios on the factors that people had identified as critical, then led a discussion about connecting plans with what is important for the region. The potential impacts of these scenarios on the critical factors mentioned above are shown in Table 2.

Scenario 1 — Continue with current trends — captured the rapid expansion of the dairy industry, the role that dairy plays in supporting regional economic development, and the rising concerns about the environmental consequences of the expansion. This scenario also considered the extra pressure on infrastructure and the changes in the traditional fabric of rural communities. For example, in Southland, more than one in five jobs are provided by the dairy industry, and the dairy

Critical factors	Description
Natural resource management	Land use and environmental limits
Population demographics	Sustainable population and critical mass
Economic development	Global market signals and local industry profitability
Infrastructure	Roads, bridges, housing and information technology
Quality of life	Regional resources and opportunities for families

Table 1. Critical factors affecting future development identified by Southland workshop participants.

sector accounts for more than 15 per cent of Southland's economy. Land-use change from sheep and beef to dairy farming has been fuelled by the opportunity for both greater profitability and greater capital gains on land value, but it also requires more intensive farming, which often leads to an increased environmental footprint. In this scenario, environmental, institutional and social resilience would be under the most pressure, as economic resilience is prioritised.

Scenario 2 — Environmental limits — considered the setting of environmental limits under the National Policy Statement for Freshwater Management (NPS-FM). This policy requires either short-term or medium-term action in response to water quality issues and has implications for production and growth in the region. Under this scenario, the implementation of good management practices is essential and, in some cases, may require additional infrastructure or even a shift in farm systems to manage nutrient losses and emissions within agreed limits. All of these may have implications for farm profitability and land value, which may change the competitiveness of current land uses. In this scenario, economic and institutional resilience would be under the most pressure, as environmental resilience is prioritised.

Scenario 3 — Diversification of land use — involved exploring the impacts of diversifying land use and attempts by enterprises within the region to address sustainable economic, social, environmental and cultural well-being of the rural community (e.g. vegetable production, new leasing agreements and co-op farming). These examples represent a significant change from current land-use trends; thinking 'outside the box' was required, particularly in cases where land was too fragmented and isolated to farm. This scenario has the potential to add value to current livestock businesses and create new farming systems for the region. It takes a holistic approach that would aim to increase all types of resilience but may compromise economic resilience in the short term while changes are being undertaken.

The workshops helped participants to develop an appreciation of other stakeholders' visions for their community and created an environment for ongoing interaction. This approach is good for discussing complicated issues and policies, which can have trade-offs and unintended consequences.

The Rural Futures Multi-Agent Simulation (RF-MAS) model (see Chapter 6) also proved to be an excellent tool to provide real-time demonstrations to community members. This helped to show how the many factors influencing sustainable agriculture affected the desired outcomes. Specifically, it moved the discussion towards concrete and quantified measures of social, environmental and economic resilience. Participants agreed the exercise had been worthwhile by either providing new knowledge or giving them plenty of food for thought; it helped them to look ahead and attempt to qualify and quantify the wider implications of changes in land use.

Agent-based modelling

The development of tools and processes to help New Zealand's pastoral industries achieve highly productive and sustainable farming has been at the heart of the Resilient Rural Communities programme. The relationships between production, economics, society and environment are fundamentally complex, and agent-based modelling is not a magic potion, but, as elegantly stated by a couple of expert economists from the US, 'when it comes to policy predictions, the models in use are not wrong, they are simply non-existent'.[7]

So far we have used this modelling to address a variety of region-wide issues and challenges, most of which surfaced during the workshops. These challenges included addressing the following issues in Southland:

• Potential impacts of water-related policies and land use, water quality, and nitrogen loss mitigation practices.[8]

Critical factors	Scenario		
	1. Continue with current trends	2. Set environmental limits	3. Diversify land use
Natural resource management	x	✓	✓
Population demographics	x	✓	✓
Economic development	✓	✓/x	✓
Infrastructure	Driven by priorities	Driven by priorities	Unsure what it may look like
Quality of life	✓	✓	✓

Table 2. A comparison of the three possible scenarios for Southland across the dimensions mentioned in Table 1. A tick represents a positive impact on the critical factors identified as important for sustainable development and a cross represents a negative impact.

- An assessment of the cost and effectiveness of mitigation measures to reduce nitrogen and phosphorus losses and greenhouse gas emissions from pastoral farms.[9]
- The economic and environmental implications of a potential expansion of the dairy sector in the region.[10]
- The implications of removing palm kernel expeller (PKE) as a feed source for dairy cows.[11]

Freshwater policies —

Setting water quality and water-use regulations is a key principle of the NPS-FM. We used the agent-based model to explore the choices farmers would make in changing land use if policy was to set a cap on nitrogen losses. Typical land use and management across dairy, sheep and beef, and forestry were modelled for a baseline season (2011/12), then the RF-MAS model estimated both extent of land-use change and management change 25 years into the future with different nitrogen leaching loss limits.

Practices to reduce the environmental impacts of each farm type (sheep and beef, and dairy) were grouped or bundled by cost and ease of adoption and were identified as 'improved nutrient management' (low capital investment, easiest to adopt), 'improved animal productivity' (intermediate cost and ease of adoption), and 'restricted grazing' (high capital investment, hardest to adopt). The main outcomes of these scenarios were:

- Sheep and beef farms were barely constrained by the caps because of their lower nitrogen leaching losses.
- Land area under dairying depended on nitrogen leaching policy:
  - Dairying increased when the annual allowable nitrogen leaching losses were 45 kilograms nitrogen per hectare or higher.
  - Dairying decreased when the annual allowable nitrogen leaching losses were 30 kilograms nitrogen per hectare or lower.

Dairy expansion has changed the look of
Southland and created new challenges for
sustainable farming with increasing pressure on
the region's land and water resources.

Some of the implications of using different mitigation bundles to reduce environmental footprint are as follows:

- Sheep and beef farms could reduce annual nitrogen leaching losses by about 30 per cent, but the adoption of practices to do so will reduce profit by 5 to 65 per cent, depending on the mitigation bundle chosen.
- Dairy farms grew more feed and used more inputs, produced more animal product, and leached about two to three times more nitrogen than sheep and beef farms.
- A modest reduction in annual nitrogen leaching losses on both medium-intensity (up to about 20 per cent) and high-intensity (up to about 30 per cent) dairy farms can be achieved with a slight increase in profit (less than 10 per cent).
- In order to reduce annual nitrogen leaching losses to 20 kilograms nitrogen per hectare or less on dairy farms, expensive measures must be adopted, reducing farm profitability by about 15 per cent (medium-intensity dairy farms) or 20 per cent (high-intensity dairy farms).

Potential expansion of the dairy sector —
Southland could potentially expand its area under dairying to about 46 per cent of its agricultural land. To explore the impact of this expansion, we simulated the conversion of current arable sheep and beef farms to dairy. More dairy farming led to a substantial increase in regional profit, but this came at an environmental cost (increased nitrogen leaching losses and greenhouse gas emissions) without considering the option of other profitable land uses as opposed to dairying.

The shift in land use since the 1990s has come with increased pressures on the region's land and water resources, to the extent that the quality of freshwater bodies (including the Waituna Lagoon) across the region has dropped. This is likely to be a response to both more dairying and more intensive land use across all sectors and those parts of the landscape where additional stress has been placed on these resources.

Dairying without PKE —

Growing consumer awareness relating to the consequences of indigenous deforestation linked to palm oil production may increase pressure to find alternatives to PKE. Farm systems intensification has recently included a growing use of this imported supplement; workshop attendees questioned this practice and highlighted the risk to the region from the growing reliance on PKE. What would no PKE mean for farms and the region? We used the RF-MAS model to explore the potential impacts on two dairy farm production systems (mid-intensity and high-intensity dairy systems), and tested the implications of:

- immediate removal of PKE; feed inputs were reduced, causing a reduction in milk production, and
- removal of PKE in one to two years; this allowed time for the substitution of PKE with suitable feed alternatives.

We found that mid-intensity dairy farms were more resilient to the removal of PKE compared with high-intensity farms. Faced with the need to remove PKE as a feed source, farmers would benefit from reducing cow numbers, with the same production per cow, rather than carrying the same number of cows and dropping per-cow production. Also, substantial amounts of barley grain (chosen here as a potential PKE replacer) would need to be transported into the region or produced locally to replace PKE. This highlights the increased vulnerability of the farm system when it is reliant on external resources. As a result, it shows the complexity of resilience: economic and environmental impacts depend on the mix between farming intensity and how much off-farm inputs are available.

The modelling approach used in all cases above provided a framework that can be extended to other regions to accommodate different farming systems and capture the interactions between farm types, land-use capabilities and farming options. More detail on the results of the RF-MAS modelling is provided in Chapter 6.

Southland is a region experiencing ongoing changes in land-use and population dynamics. The rapid expansion of dairying has had implications for a range of stakeholders and resources in the community with differing values. The strategies to manage these values prioritise different resilience dimensions, and the use of participatory workshops with stakeholders helps to consider them. Linking of modelling tools and regional land resource information was important for demonstrating likely changes in land use, economics and environmental impacts for the entire region under different regulations, constraints and pressures.

The participatory workshops, along with the RF-MAS model, provided a dynamic platform for stakeholders to explore scenarios and their potential implications at farm and industry level and work collaboratively to address local and regional issues.

One of the key findings from the workshops and analysis is that Southland has options for increasing its resilience. For example, it can reduce its use of off-farm inputs such as PKE, but that has implications for the intensity of dairy farming. In turn, the extent and intensity of dairy farming has wider implications for the region. The scenarios considered in the workshops had implications for the factors that Southlanders themselves had identified as critical. Balancing these factors and supporting future resilience is a continuing conversation.

Chapter 10 —

How will technology affect the fabric of rural communities?

— *Bruce Small*

Resilience is future oriented, and it is more achievable when people are prepared. Understanding the nature of potential changes can help us to prepare for them, enabling greater choice and control over our futures and over outcomes associated with changes that are beyond our control.

This chapter is intended for those policy-makers responsible for rural development strategies in national and regional government, and rural businesses, rural residents and rural communities. Having technological foresight (planning with a view to future technologies) gives rural actors an increased ability to control and mitigate undesirable impacts, adapt to changing circumstances, and capitalise on any new transformative opportunities emanating from these technologies.

Technological developments that could impact significantly on agriculture and rural life are undoubtedly on the way. Understanding the potential of these emerging technologies and their adoption and use by (and/or acceptability to) producers, consumers and communities is vital information for rural resilience and strategic decision-making that benefits the agricultural sector.

Upcoming disruptive technologies

Future changes range from the highly probable to the highly uncertain to the completely unpredictable. And while built-in system redundancy, constant vigilance, reflection, reflexivity and adaptive management are the primary approaches to managing an unanticipated future, it is nonetheless difficult to prepare for the completely unpredictable.

Such change is not the topic of this chapter, however. Instead, the chapter explains the issues and forces that influence global agriculture and discusses two emerging technologies that could help to address these issues: the digital revolution and synthetic food production. These technologies could also radically change or disrupt existing rural enterprises, rural lifestyles and the New Zealand agricultural sector. We consider what these technologies might mean for rural enterprises and rural lives and how they might interact with each other.

While predictions can be fraught with uncertainty, there are windows through which the future may be glimpsed. First, we can consider the forces and issues that are shaping the future of agriculture both globally and nationally — the context of global modern agriculture. Second, by observing new technologies and innovative business models emerging from high-technology enclaves such as Silicon Valley, we can glimpse the future decade unveiling as these technologies and practices spread across the globe.

It has been argued by futurists such as Alvin Toffler, Raymond Kurzweil and Bill Gates that knowledge, science and technology develop at an exponential, rather than a linear, rate — that is, more and more rapidly over time. Exponential growth occurs in several stages of technological development: science discovery, performance improvement, miniaturisation and price reduction.

Rapid developments in digital agriculture and synthetic food technologies indicate that the elbow of the exponential curve has been entered and the pace of development of these technologies will accelerate rapidly. The next two to three decades might see a revolution in food production that was almost as dramatic as the shift from nomadic hunter-gathering to agricultural societies.

The context of modern global agriculture

To start, we provide some context about agriculture and food that explains why farming is heading towards a different future.

The need for more food —

In 1961 the world's population was 3.07 billion. In the next 50 years the global population more than doubled to 7.01 billion. The main response to the increased food demand was the taking of land and water for the intensification of agriculture. During this time, the increased production of animal products accounted for 65 per cent of land-use change and agriculture was the primary driver of land-use change.[1]

The global population is projected to rise to around 9.8 billion by 2050. Global middle-class numbers are projected to increase from 3.2 billion in 2016 to 5.2 billion by 2030. As people have become wealthier, traditionally they have increased their consumption of animal products — in particular, meat, milk and eggs; the global meat demand is projected to increase by 73 per cent between 2011 and 2050.[2]

The environment and agriculture —

The green revolution, established in the 1960s to increase productivity through genetic gain and through fertiliser, pesticide and herbicide use, was remarkably successful in feeding the world's growing population; however, it came at a high cost. Concern is growing about the environmental effects of the expansion of agricultural land use and increasing agricultural intensity. In 2011 agriculture occupied around 50 per cent of the world's habitable land surface; animal production used 69 per cent of agricultural land and the average agricultural area available per person was 0.65 hectares.

Agriculture has significant negative impacts on soil: 50 per cent of the world's topsoil has been lost in the past 150 years and 40 per cent of the world's agricultural land is seriously degraded. Soil erosion is currently occurring at up to 300 times the rate of natural renewal and this will present a problem for future food production.[3]

Seventy per cent of the world's supply of fresh water is used for agriculture; it is being extracted at an unsustainable rate and rivers, lakes and aquifers are depleting rapidly. This in itself is a major threat to the sustainable development of human society; however, fertilisers, pesticides, herbicides, antibiotics and livestock also make agriculture a major source of water pollution, which threatens ecosystems and human health and constrains economic activity.[4]

In addition, agricultural expansion is fuelling unprecedented deforestation, which is a major cause of species extinction and bio-diversity loss. With the current rate of species loss estimated to be up to 100 times the background rates of the past 60 million years, biologists are referring to this rapid depletion of biodiversity as the sixth great extinction event. Agriculture is a significant contributor to this impending biodiversity catastrophe.[5]

Agricultural practices are a major contributor to climate change. Globally, livestock are directly responsible for 12 per cent of all greenhouse gas (GHG) pollution (17 per cent in New Zealand) and, when combined with land-use change and indirect agricultural emissions (e.g.

New technologies such as large-scale
irrigation have changed land-use options
in many parts of New Zealand.

agrochemical production and fossil fuel use), agriculture is estimated to account for between 17 and 32 per cent of all GHG emissions caused by humans. A consequence of global warming is sea-level rise, which will remove valuable agricultural land from production and further exacerbate the growing demand for agricultural land.

Ethics and agriculture —

Current agricultural production and distribution raises moral questions.

First, the land resource required to feed the average person from the developed world (US = 1.8 hectare per person) and the average person from the developing world (India = 0.3 hectare per person) reveals a vast social inequity. Developed-world diets are rich in land-intensive animal foods. However, overnutrition is a growing dietary problem, with approximately 2.1 billion people classified as obese and a prevalence of associated health problems, such as diabetes and heart disease. In the developing world, in which less land-intensive food is consumed, malnutrition and undernutrition affect more than 795 million people.[6]

A second moral issue for a growing number of people concerns humans' use of animals and the welfare and slaughter of those animals. Humans farm and kill 56–70 billion animals per year (excluding fish) to eat; based on present trends, this rate is expected to double by 2050. A considerable number of these animals are farmed in conditions with little respect for their welfare.

As the public comes to understand morally questionable environmental and animal farming practices, local communities may not be free to operate as they like. First-world consumers are viewing the production and distribution of food from a more ethical perspective; these consumers want a food supply that is secure, healthy and nutritious; tastes good; respects the dignity and welfare of animals; and has a benign environmental footprint. Driven by environmental and animal ethics concerns, there is an increasing appetite around the world for vegetarian and vegan diets.

Although current agricultural practices are producing sufficient quantities of food for the world, they are failing to do so either sustainably or in a manner that lives up to the demanding criteria of the emerging modern ethical consumer. Current practices will be unable to supply food to a world of 9.8 billion people; attempting to do so will worsen already unsustainable environmental degradation. In order to feed the world in 2050 sustainably, transformative and revolutionary approaches to food production are required.

Digital technologies and digital agriculture
Digital technologies are affecting agriculture and rural communities. Digital agriculture refers to farm management technologies that integrate remote sensors (e.g. satellites and drones) or embedded sensors with cloud computing and artificial intelligence to provide tools for improving farmer decision-making and increasing farm automation and production efficiency.

On farm, these technologies are married to precision agriculture machinery and practices. Precision agriculture is an information technology approach to farm management designed to ensure that crops and soil receive exactly what they need for optimum health and productivity.

However, digital agriculture extends well beyond the farm gate; it permeates the entire food value chain. With digital data available for all value-chain sectors and processes, communication with value chain partners such as suppliers and customers may be carried out electronically, with data transmission, processing and analysis for the most part being automated.

Many major businesses, as well as innovative start-ups, are developing these technologies for agricultural use. These include The Climate Corporation, John Deere, Monsanto, DuPont, Nufarm, WinField United, SST Software, MapShots, Raven Products, Trimble, AgGateway, AgSolver,

Aglink, Delta Agribusiness, Precision Agriculture, Hortus Technical Services, Conservis and Ag Leader.

A range of new or soon-to-emerge digital technologies will help to enable digital agriculture. These include GPS-guided and precision-delivery farm machinery (e.g. water, fertiliser, pesticides), agricultural robots, universal mobile broadband, wireless sensors and the internet of things (IoT), cloud computing, artificial intelligence (AI) and machine learning, sustainable energy generation and storage, 3D printing, nanotechnology and material science, biotechnology and blockchain technology.

Digital technologies offer ways of addressing some of the unsustainability issues associated with agriculture. Sensors will enable precise mapping and reporting of animals, crops and fields, while decision software and AI devices (AIs) will determine where and when water, fertiliser and pesticides are needed and will control farm machinery to deliver precise quantities as required. This could help to reduce agricultural water use and environmental pollution, while maximising yields and reducing input costs for farmers.

It is anticipated that human agriculturalists will be assisted initially by AIs with decision-making and management options, with the various aspects of farming being automated progressively over time, reducing on-farm labour. Increasingly, however, farmers may take on governance roles. The demand for labour could also be reduced along the agricultural value chain as AIs take the jobs of logistics planners, accountants, lawyers, market analysts, vehicles drivers and labourers.

Digital technologies also offer a mechanism for transparency throughout the agricultural value chain. Sensors and blockchain technology enable a true and immutable record of all digital data recorded throughout a product's life cycle. Such data could be used for quality audit and compliance purposes, as well as traceability for proof of responsible production and product provenance and as a mechanism to tell a product's market story.

Smart contracts, powered by blockchain technology, will securely automate internet business transactions and do away with the need for intermediaries or independent third parties, thus providing a mechanism for shortened value chains and perhaps enabling direct producer-to-consumer marketing.

Given the drive towards digital agriculture by major players and innovators, combined with the increasing power of digital technologies and the need to increase the efficiency, sustainability and productivity of agriculture, it is only a matter of time before digital technologies are adopted across the agricultural sector. Many of these technologies will sustain current on-farm agricultural production, making agriculture incrementally more efficient. Eventually, it may be possible to automate agriculture and food distribution completely, although this is by no means on the immediate horizon.

The disruptive potential of digital agriculture is related primarily to system change throughout the entire agricultural supply chain and to human labour both on farm and along the value chain. New skills and labour may be required both on and off farm to maintain and manage the machines and software.

Emerging and maturing digital technologies may also impact significantly on those living in rural communities. Digital technologies collapse space and time, bringing rural communities closer to the rest of the world through instant communication and helping to alleviate rural isolation. A range of new activities and services in health, recreation and entertainment, education, and social and political participation will open up to rural community members.

Perhaps the most truly transformative aspect of digital technologies will be the way in which they impact on human lifestyles and, for rural communities in particular, the integration of community members into the wider social world. As the isolation of rural life is removed, rural communities may attract new residents who are refugees from unaffordable urban housing markets and who may now find meaningful, non-agricultural occupations and lifestyles in rural areas.

Cellular agriculture and plant-based substitutes for animal products

A revolution is beginning in food production through the advent of cellular agriculture and plant-based animal product substitutes; that is, food made in the laboratory or factory and food made almost entirely without animals and farms.

Cellular agriculture and plant-based animal substitutes represent a truly disruptive and transformative technology to the current agricultural production system. The start-up companies in high-technology enclaves that are developing these technologies are being funded generously by technology billionaires such as Richard Branson, Bill Gates and Sergey Brin, and even by traditional agricultural giants such as Tyson Foods and Cargill.

Cultured milk —

A Silicon Valley company, Perfect Day, is making milk without cows. The process uses genetically engineered yeast to bio-brew milk in vats. The technology is very similar to the process that uses genetically engineered bacteria to make insulin for diabetics or beer, which is brewed in a similar fashion. The milk can be adjusted so that those with dairy allergies are able to consume it. It may also be fortified with other vitamins or nutrients to enhance its health-giving potential.

Perfect Day claims its dairy products are vegan, soy-free, gluten-free and lactose-free and provide the same nutritional benefits, taste, texture and functionality as traditional dairy products. Once in full-scale production, it is likely that the price of the cultured milk will fall rapidly and become significantly cheaper than cow-derived milk. Products such as cheese, yogurt and ice cream can be produced from cultured milk.

Cell-cultured meat —

In cellular agriculture, animal products (e.g. meat) are grown in factories from cells taken from animals. Cellular agriculture makes products that are composed of animal cells and claim to be the molecular equivalent of the animal products. However, only harmless biopsies to obtain the starter cells are required, rather than animal slaughter.

Following the production of the first cell-cultured hamburger patty in 2013, cellular agriculture is being trialled in the production of beef, sheep, pork, turkey, chicken and fish. Eventually, cellular agriculture may produce meat that is indistinguishable from, and cheaper than, traditionally grown meat. When these conditions occur, price-sensitive commodity market segments may open up for cellular products.

Modern Meadow is a Boston-based company developing lab-cultured animal meat and leather products. Memphis Meats is a company based in San Francisco making hotdogs, sausages, burgers and meatballs from the cultured cells of cows, pigs and chickens. Mosa Meat, based in the Netherlands, and SuperMeat and Future Meat Technologies, both based in Israel, are also researching and developing similar cell-cultured meat products.

San Francisco-based Finless Foods plans to bring the cell-cultured revolution to seafood and hopes that cell-cultured bluefin tuna fillets will reach the market by 2019.

While commercial-scale production of cell-cultured meats is touted by industry optimists for 2021, it may be some years before these products affect New Zealand's commodity market share.

Plant-based protein alternatives —

Plant-based protein products contain no animal cells but may resemble animal products to varying degrees of fidelity. Some products, known as animal simulacra, attempt a very high fidelity to animal products (i.e. they try to be indistinguishable); others offer their own unique tastes and characteristics while substituting for meat. Plant-based animal simulacra are available and making strong headway into traditional meat markets.

Impossible Foods, based in Redmond, California, makes a plant-based synthetic burger patty and, as a corporate value, aims to 'reduce the environmental harm caused by unsustainable agriculture'. Beyond Meat is a Los Angeles company that manufactures plant-based burger patties and 'chicken' strips. Their corporate mission is to 'create mass-market solutions that perfectly replace animal protein with plant protein'. Another California company, New Wave Foods, aims to manufacture plant-based 'popcorn' that looks, tastes, smells and feels like real shrimp 'but without the slave labour'. The European supermarket chain Tesco recently launched a 100 per cent plant-based 'steak' product from the Dutch vegetarian and vegan food specialist Vivera.

In New Zealand, Sunfed Foods produces 'chicken-free chicken' from pea protein, rice bran oil, pea fibre, pumpkin, natural yeast extract and maize starch. Founder and chief executive Sharma Lee claims the product is soy-free, gluten-free, preservative-free, GMO-free, cholesterol-free and trans-fat-free.

Potential environmental benefits —
The companies developing and manufacturing cellular agricultural products and animal simulacra all claim significant environmental benefits over agricultural production of similar products. A life-cycle analysis by Perfect Day indicated its cellular milk production results in 84 per cent lower GHG emissions and uses 90 per cent less water, 65 per cent less energy and 90–98 per cent less land than traditional milk production. Two anticipatory life-cycle analyses conducted on cell-cultured meat found a 78–96 per cent reduction in GHG emissions, 82–96 per cent lower water consumption and 90 per cent less land use in comparison with conventional agriculture.

Threats or opportunities?

These new food production technologies offer the potential to vastly reduce the environmental impacts of agriculture, in terms of both pollution and resource extraction, thus improving sustainability and environmental resilience. They also offer the potential to ramp up food production to meet future population demands, thus increasing social resilience.

Cellular food can be manufactured in very clean environments, helping to eliminate many of the pathogens, antibiotics and hormones found in real meat and milk and thus enhancing food safety. The elimination of these things has other incidental benefits, such as reducing antimicrobial resistance. Apart from these advantages, cellular agriculture may also help to provide food security by enabling the production of food in close proximity to the major markets, thus also eliminating food mile GHG production.

The companies developing these products are receiving funding from the most visionary and wealthiest entrepreneurs in the high-technology sector of Silicon Valley. They are redefining the boundaries of what food is, how it is produced and what it means. They are also redefining the moral boundaries of food and food production and attacking traditional agricultural production by exploiting its current moral, environmental and production weaknesses.

These changes will result in large disruptions to our current farms and communities because New Zealand's market is focused on traditional agriculture and the commodity market. As such, these changes may initially disrupt resilience trajectories — some negatively, some positively.

The threat or opportunity (depending on one's perspective) is that, within 25–30 years, the bulk of commodity milk and meat could be produced without agriculture or animals and rural agriculture could potentially be reduced significantly. Environmental resilience is likely to be enhanced because less land will be required for farming. Whether economic resilience increases or decreases will depend upon the ability of the agricultural sector to mitigate and adapt or recognise and seize arising opportunities.

Globally, synthetic food production could produce enormous benefits for the environment and for non-human animal species. Such a change could impact significantly on New Zealand, affecting not only our agriculture but also our economy, environment and rural life. If New Zealand's agriculture manages to adapt and survive, resilience across all dimensions could be increased because the system would be more sustainable.

What should New Zealand do to prepare for the rapidly advancing synthetic food revolution? When cost, safety, quality and food security for the production of synthetic agricultural commodities surpasses traditional agricultural production, being in the business of producing agricultural commodities could be extremely challenging. What will the market for high-quality traditional agricultural products look like when synthetic food is commodified? What product attributes will the 'real food' market segment demand?

Clearly, moving away from production of low-value agricultural commodities will be highly desirable. Because New Zealand's contribution to the world food supply is a relative drop in the ocean, a better and more sustainable strategy may be to focus on the production of high-quality, value-added 'real' or 'natural' agricultural products aimed at higher-end markets. Wealthy 'real food' consumers will likely demand products of the highest nutritional quality, safety and ethical production. They will also demand complete traceability, transparency of production and a guarantee of authenticity and provenance.

The adoption of digital agriculture will help to reduce the environmental impacts of conventional agriculture, establish producer–consumer relationships, provide traceability, and guarantee product quality, provenance and market story. As such, digital agriculture will be an important cornerstone and prerequisite for New Zealand agriculture's successful adaptation to the synthetic food marketplace. In preparation for this coming future, the New Zealand agricultural sector needs to change its current focus from high-volume production to high-quality, high-value and environmentally sustainable produce.

New Zealand will not be the only traditional agricultural producer targeting wealthy markets with real food: competition will be strong. New Zealand has a reputational advantage for producing healthy food in a clean, green, natural environment; over the next two decades it will be imperative to maintain this status and reputation. Care will be required to ensure that the current drive for intensified production does not impact negatively on animal welfare and our environment, potentially damaging New Zealand's strategic and reputational advantage.

For New Zealand agriculture to be resilient in the face of future technologies, we need to ensure that the pathway to capturing the opportunity resident in these future high-value markets is not closed off for short-term gain. The more natural, organic and environmentally clean the New Zealand agricultural sector can genuinely claim to be, and the higher the quality of agricultural products, the better positioned the sector will be to complement the commodity synthetic food market with high-value, conventionally produced 'real foods'.

4. How will these changes be integrated?

___

Outdoor recreation activities, such as cycling on the growing network of trails throughout the country, provide opportunities for entrepreneurship on New Zealand's family farms, from food and accommodation to locally made produce and crafts.

4.

Chapter 11 —

Entrepreneurship on New Zealand family farms

— Tracy Nelson and Mike Mackay

In a feature story in the 2016 March/April edition of *NZ Life & Leisure*, journalist Cheree Morrison offers the story of Westmere Farm: the 'home, business and playground' of the Laugesen-Campbell family.[1]

The property, which is in the Waitaki Valley of New Zealand's South Island, is a dynamic and multifaceted family business, comprising an 1100-hectare irrigated dairy operation, a Wagyu beef-raising enterprise and a lavender venture, involving the growing, harvesting, processing and selling of home-crafted products at a small retail outlet located on the property.

While the magazine article presents a light-hearted account of everyday life on the farm, it also tells the story of a family that has created, through innovative entrepreneurial experimentation, a diverse farm business portfolio while also contributing to a wider set of family and community values. Similar accounts of farm diversification are easy to locate in the popular media, where they reinforce a picture of New Zealand farmers as resilient innovators who embody the can-do spirit of the nation.

While the entrepreneurial adventures of New Zealand farmers remain a popular media theme, rural researchers have not displayed the same (sustained) level of interest in the topic. Rural research in New Zealand has, for the most part, focused on the development of large-scale monofunctional farms, and on the rise of key industry sectors, such as dairying, that produce the bulk of the nation's export earnings along with some of its most pressing environmental challenges.

To balance the ledger, in this chapter we present a set of case studies of new enterprise creation on family-owned pastoral farms in New Zealand. The properties we analyse are spaces of conventional pastoral agriculture (sheep, beef and dairy farming) and sites of innovative entrepreneurial experimentation, involving at least one of food processing, on-farm retailing, agritourism, accommodation, environmental education and commercial outdoor recreation.

While our research began with multiple objectives in mind, our aim in this chapter is to report *why* our research participants had diversified, or were diversifying, their farm businesses. Although drawn from only a small sample of farms, our findings point to entanglements of economic and social motives in the decisions to create new farm ventures. They demonstrate the connections between the dimensions of resilience on farms and in rural communities.

The changing face of farm entrepreneurship

There is limited integrated research available on the entrepreneurial experiences of farming families in New Zealand. The exception is a set of studies conducted in the 1990s and located within an argument over New Zealand farmers' responses to rural restructuring, crisis and change.[2]

The context for that research was the removal of long-standing farm subsidies and the deregulation and reregulation of the primary industries (a process that began in 1984). At the time, the removal of agricultural subsidies was a major concern for New Zealand farmers — it had an immediate and mostly negative effect on farm income and debt levels and the capacity to employ outside labour. The situation led to a wave of interest in the coping strategies of New Zealand farmers; the focus was on how farmers would adapt, transform and bounce forward.

One strategy reported was for members of the family to seek employment from the farm to generate much-needed supplementary farm income.[3] Another strategy was to diversify into new forms of on-farm economic activity: these included tourism, but also new variants of agricultural and horticultural production, food and beverage processing, light manufacturing, and agricultural services and consultancy.

Taylor et al.[4] suggest that the common creation of these 'alternative' farm enterprises was a strategy to diversify farm income streams and, by extension, restore the long-term viability of the family farm. For this reason, the initial 'flowering'[5] of rural entrepreneurship in New Zealand was interpreted mainly as an economic survival strategy.

In recent years, however, a very different picture of farm entre-preneurship has emerged, placing it at the centre of debates about the globalising economy — a process that is creating new opportunities for farmers in New Zealand and abroad.[6] When seen in this more positive light, farm entrepreneurship emerges as a proactive form of engagement with new market opportunities, rather than action born of economic necessity.

Woods examines this phenomenon in a number of case studies from the UK, Australia and New Zealand,[7] emphasising farmer choice, or how 'globally engaged' family farmers are deploying their business acumen,

Farmers' markets have become increasingly popular around New Zealand, and are an example of the social 'glue' that can support resilience in rural communities. They are also great marketing and retail opportunities for the products of rural entrepreneurship.

	Farm 1	Farm 2
Type of new venture	Raw milk and locally made cheeses sold direct to consumer	Eco-education, luxury eco-lodge and outdoor recreation activities
Start of new venture	2014	2012
Main farm system	Dairy (irrigated)	Sheep and beef
Size of farm	260-hectare milking platform (large dairy farm)	610 hectares (medium sheep and beef farm)
Location	North Island, close to urban centre; major dairy region	North Island, remote area; prominent area for viticulture, horticulture, and sheep and beef
Involved persons (family)	Couple (husband and wife), and adult daughter	Couple (husband and wife) and school-aged children
Number of employees in new enterprise (not family)	Three full-time	Two full-time (also WWOOFers)

Table 1. Details of the five case-study farms.

Farm 3	Farm 4	Farm 5
B&B/tourist lodgings (six glamping huts)	Value-added/farm-branded meat sold direct to consumer	Sheep-milk cheese production and retailing
2008	2015	2000
Dairy grazing and beef	Beef	Sheep
251 hectares (medium grazing unit)	600 hectares (medium beef farm)	15 hectares (+ leasing more land in the district)
South Island, semi-remote rural area; dairy growth zone	North Island, semi-remote rural area; well-established dairy zone	South Island, close to urban area and prominent tourism area and setting for lifestyle block development
Couple (but mainly wife) and school-aged children	One (daughter of farm owners)	Couple (husband and wife), and young adult children
Two local people on casual/on-call basis	None	One full-time, plus two in the shop located off farm

local–global networks and resources to develop new and diverse on-farm businesses.

In this chapter, we begin exploring the key elements of entrepreneurial activity on New Zealand farms through a small number of business cases. The five businesses chosen show how, unlike the element of survival associated with the rise of new farm ventures in New Zealand in the 1980s and '90s, farmers are engaging in entrepreneurship in an entirely new context and for very different reasons.

Diversifying farms case studies

We found our five case-study farms by searching the internet and rural print media. They are both self-defined family farms and multifunctional properties; that is, they comprise a conventional farming operation — dairy, sheep, beef and/or grazing — and at least one new enterprise.

As seen in Table 1, these farms show different farm types and sizes and cover a wide range of new enterprise developments. This includes niche food processing and direct sales, tourism accommodation, agritourism, events, education, novel dairy and niche red meat processing, packaging and distribution.

We explored these farms first by talking with each farming family about the farm's history and the development of their new businesses, then by walking around the farms to see the operations in practice.

Why our farmers diversified

Our research participants were archetypal entrepreneurs: they had all identified market opportunities and, through elements of risk-taking and capital investment, brought the ideas to fruition. Many of them attested to being competitive in nature, having eyed opportunities to test themselves against other farmers — often their friends — who had successfully diversified their economic practices.

In discussing their reasons for developing their new farm ventures, all our interviewees outlined a mix of economic, environmental and lifestyle goals, combined with a somewhat more instrumental desire to do more with their land and existing farm capacity (e.g. surplus household labour, resources, and business and agricultural knowledge).

On the economic side of the ledger, all our farmers characterised their decisions to diversify as ways of developing more sustainable, and therefore future-proofed, family businesses. None of them urgently needed the income generated from the additional ventures — their farms were already profitable — but they all recognised that their decisions to diversify had created more agile and viable business portfolios, providing future options should the situations of the main farm businesses change.

In discussing this, our participants were quick to point out that the main farm enterprises were not subsidising each new venture, which had to be a self-sustaining and profitable business that, as one farmer put it, 'had to stand on its own two feet'.

Questions of farm succession also featured in our research participants' reasons to diversify. All the farmers we interviewed had children ranging from school age to young adulthood, some of whom worked on the property, while others had left home. Most of our interviewees hoped that one or more of their children would one day decide to stay on or return to and take ownership of the property, but were realistic in their thinking, aware that some of their offspring were not interested in farming per se.

In several cases, farmers characterised their new farm ventures as their way of creating new career options for their children on the property but outside of farming, thus potentially increasing the role of kin in the business and ultimately maintaining the legacy of the family farm. As three of our entrepreneurial farmers put it, 'part of the thrill is the new succession possibilities . . . rather than having our son or daughter take on the farm, there's now the opportunity for them to be involved in marketing or communications — endless opportunities!'

'When you have children, you start thinking about the future a bit more. You join the dots together about where everything is heading and think about things like sustainability. So you sit and ask yourself, how can I make the farm a better place for them? We're not hung up on our kids being farmers, but we'd like them to be here in some capacity and the place now offers choices.'

'My daughter and son help. I want them to have ownership of the new [business] because it might be theirs in five to 10 years . . . it's cool to have built a new option for their future.'

The farmers who participated in our research also described their new ventures in terms of 'challenging projects' that created important sources of satisfaction for themselves and their wider families. Most of them spoke of the gratification they derived from planning the new businesses, discussing options, doing the research and steering the projects to completion.

In all cases, the creation of the new ventures required the application and honing of new skills, placing many farmers outside their comfort zones but ultimately extending their horizons. This was an exciting prospect.

'We have always been passionate cooks, and we're also both keen foodies, so the new business [the farm lodge] has given us the chance to try our hand at those things. We have food waiting for them [the visitors to the farm] when they arrive!'

'I really needed a new project, something I could build from scratch and involve the family in. I really wanted to do something that taught my children that money doesn't grow on trees and that they should seize every opportunity without regret. I think everybody needs a challenging project on the go . . . it's good for self-improvement and confidence building.'

Several of the farmers we spoke to said they enjoyed engaging in new farm-based activities simply because this allowed them to find reprieves from the everyday demands of conventional farm work, and achieve a new and positive sense of direction, as in the case of the following interviewees:

'Farming is hard, and so is life on the farm, so the new business became my happy place.'

'I was getting a bit bored with farming, so we got something up and running that was a bit different.'

Enhancing social contact was another reason our farmers gave for starting their new farm enterprises. This was a particularly important motive for the participants who lived in relatively isolated settings and those who had developed agritourism/accommodation ventures. These farmers spoke fondly of their interactions with visitors and tourists, which included such activities as walking the farm together, engaging in farm tasks, sharing stories and sitting down to enjoy meals together. The following quote from a North Island farmer illustrates the point:

'I always found farming a bit of a lonely activity, but now we've always got something different going on around the place and different people to connect with.'

Some of our farmers said they were determined to develop a business that reflected their love of agriculture and would help other people connect with the land. As one farmer put it:

'There is a loss of connection to nature and to food, and so we wanted our business to be a bridge — and not just to bridge the urban/rural divide but also to connect people back to the places where their food is grown and to think more about issues around food production. People come here, and they just do not want to leave — so that is a really good buzz!'

'We host school visits and so we do "school tourism"! People visiting or staying here, even Kiwi families, love to come and feed the chooks and drink some fresh milk. We can show them how we look after the animals, recycle products, and capture effluent and use it again on the farm. So educating others about farming is a big part of the whole thing.'

Another farmer wanted his business to reflect his environmental ethic and wanted also to build a similar ethos in others:

'We wanted to show the world that we were restoring ecosystems on our farm and employing models of sustainable agriculture. So we opened up the farm, and that's where the lodge idea came from — it allows people to come on to the land and stay on the farm. We even have planting opportunities for them, and walking tracks out through the native forest and around the lake.'

Insights for future farm entrepreneurship studies

One of the intentions of our research was to allow farmers to explain, in their own terms, the reasons they developed their new farm ventures. Their retrospective stories suggest that it is difficult for them to untangle the lifestyle and economic dimensions of their entrepreneurial activities — both are evident in all five of our case studies.

Our findings, while drawn from only a small sample of farms, suggest that economic, environmental and lifestyle choices are always part of farmers' motives to develop new enterprises. We therefore advocate for a 'both/and' approach to the study and interpretation of farm entrepreneurship.

While the prime focus of our research was on motives, our qualitative approach also produced rich material around the challenges of creating new farm ventures for farmers. These insights provide future directions for studies of farm entrepreneurship in New Zealand.

One issue identified was the difficulty in striking a balance between the often unexpected demands of the new venture and the dynamics of family life. As Jervell observes, family farms differ from other family businesses in that the farm is usually also the family home and thus is deeply intertwined with the flow and necessities of everyday life.[8]

Not surprisingly then, on our farm walks, our interviewees pointed to sites of significance for the family, such as where their children catch the rural school bus or where they themselves played as children. Thus, the farm walk elicited expressions of often multi-generational interconnectedness with places and future development plans, including their entrepreneurial aspirations. A key question then is, 'What household strategies do farmers develop and deploy in order to balance the demands of their multiple businesses with the dynamic and often demanding nature of family and community life?'

Another key challenge that emerged was the need to navigate new and often unfamiliar rules and regulations during the start-up phase of a new venture. The farmers we spoke to emphasised the importance of developing reliable and cooperative networks of support, preferably with other successful rural entrepreneurs to whom they could turn for information, encouragement and advice.

This insight points to the need for further field investigations examining the social dimension of farmer resilience and networked characteristics of farm entrepreneurship, as well as the types of support that should/could be put in place by those who would like to see farm entrepreneurship thrive.

Chapter 12 —

Increasing indigenous biodiversity in farming landscapes

— *Fleur Maseyk and Estelle Dominati*

F arms and rural communities depend on the natural environment but can also have major effects upon it. A key aspect of the environment is biodiversity and New Zealand's experience with biodiversity demonstrates the scale of these effects. As human settlement changed New Zealand's lowlands from forested habitat to a farming landscape, more than 90 per cent of the indigenous vegetation was lost.[1] Now, increasing biodiversity on farm is fundamental to protecting and enhancing the ability of farming to operate within environmental limits.

Biodiversity on farm refers to all the elements of nature — plants, animals, soil and water — found in or passing through the farming landscape. Increasing biodiversity on farm is about shifting from primarily single-use landscapes solely dedicated to food and fibre production to multi-purpose landscapes. These new landscapes can include several land covers or even land uses, including production agriculture. Such farming landscapes contain diversity across several dimensions — species, land cover and land use.

What are the benefits of increasing biodiversity?

The benefits of increasing biodiversity on farms extend across all the resilience dimensions. One obvious benefit is the amenity value of having a variety of trees across the landscape. The benefits go beyond amenity values, however. The future of agriculture in the long term relies on sustaining the capacity of all the farm's natural assets, and that includes the natural environment. By actively protecting and enhancing biodiversity on farm, farmers can also improve the perceptions of the wider, non-farming community and secure social licence to operate.

More broadly, New Zealand's plants and animals define its landscapes and provide a unique sense of place, a connection that runs through generations and connects us to the past and to the future. The potential benefits of increasing biodiversity are therefore economic, environmental, social and cultural.

Consistent with the themes in this book, it is important to understand that biodiversity doesn't just happen on farms; it is the result of choices made by farmers, communities and governments that are better or worse for biodiversity. Our work shows that there are pathways with the potential to connect farms to their broader environments and thereby increase their resilience; however, people will have to make conscious decisions to make changes. This chapter will interest people who are involved in those decisions — farmers, land managers, and local, regional and national policy-makers.

Why is indigenous biodiversity important?

Indigenous biodiversity, which refers to plant and animal species found naturally here, i.e. not brought by people, has a special place in New Zealand. It is important for resilient farms and communities as it provides the foundation for the natural productive capacity of farms and the building blocks on which to enhance existing farm assets. The vast majority of New Zealand's plant and animal species are endemic: they are found nowhere else in the world. If they are lost from New Zealand, they are simply gone forever.

New Zealand has experienced a drastic decline in indigenous biodiversity in the relatively short time since human occupation began around 1280 CE.[2] This decline includes the loss of more than 90 per cent of the country's wetlands, 60 per cent of the indigenous forest cover, and the extinction of more than 70 species. A further 40 per cent of bird species, 38 per cent of plant species, 85 per cent of lizard species and 74 per cent of freshwater fish species are currently threatened with, or at risk of, extinction.[3] Halting and reversing this decline would need a concerted effort to both protect what biodiversity of significance remains and reintroduce indigenous biodiversity in places where it has been greatly reduced.

The ongoing decline in indigenous biodiversity has severely affected the resilience of farming landscapes in changing environments. This decline can be attributed largely to historical clearance and to the present effects of pest animals and weeds that prey upon, compete with or replace indigenous species. Current land practices also play a critical part in preventing any increase in indigenous biodiversity in farming landscapes.

The suggestion that the farming landscape is not the place for indigenous biodiversity is short-sighted in that it overlooks the role of farms in the wider landscape. While it is true that an impressive 32 per cent (8.5 million hectares) of New Zealand's land area is protected as public conservation land,[4] this land is concentrated largely in the 'back country' — mountainous and hill country that is less suited to farming

Increasing indigenous biodiversity supports land
and water restoration, which in turn helps to build
resilience into farming systems.

development. The distribution percentage of protected land is stark —
above 500 metres almost half (49 per cent) of land is protected, while
below 500 metres less than one-fifth (18 per cent) of land is protected.[5]
Indigenous vegetation in lowland areas outside the reserve network has
almost completely disappeared. These lowlands comprise 23 per cent of
New Zealand's total land area and are the areas of the country that are
most suited to settlement and production.

This skewed pattern of remaining indigenous vegetation cover means
that the public conservation land inadequately preserves the full range of
New Zealand's natural diversity, with poor representation of the species
and ecosystems found at lower altitudes. This is why conservation efforts
cannot be confined to public conservation land, and farming landscapes
have an important contribution to make towards maintaining the
country's natural heritage.

Less intensively farmed hill-country farms, in particular, are already
well placed to integrate indigenous species and habitats into their daily
farm practice. This is because 25 per cent of the remaining indigenous
vegetation cover occurs on sheep and beef farms. For lowland and more
intensively farmed landscapes where indigenous vegetation is more
scarce, simply protecting and managing what is left will not be enough
to build resilience at the farm scale — the reintroduction of indigenous
vegetation will be required.

On farm, supporting biodiversity includes retaining wetlands and
remnant bush blocks, and regenerating gully vegetation and scrub on
hard-to-farm land. It also includes reintroducing woody vegetation
into the landscape, such as occurs in stabilising erosion-prone hillsides,
establishing shelter belts and planting riparian margins.

While integrating biodiversity into daily on-farm decision-making
requires additional effort, sustaining the natural environment is a key
part of building resilience. It is crucial to blur the boundaries between
the areas of the farm that produce commodities (food and fibre) and

those non-pastoral areas of the farm that produce other benefits.

Taking an ecosystems approach to farm planning provides a process with which to quantify and value the multiple benefits associated with indigenous biodiversity, link biodiversity to farm performance, and identify the management actions required to effect change. Increasing indigenous biodiversity on farm also enhances resilience; that is, the ability of farms to cope with environmental pressures, operate within social expectations and further connect farming landscapes to the wider community. Biodiversity on farm builds the capacity of natural assets to absorb the pressures of farming land uses — it provides a buffer between the farm system and critical environmental limits.

As is typical with resilience issues, the responsible management of the adverse effects of land-use practice sits not just with farmers but also with local government; district and regional councils have clear statutory responsibilities for the protection and maintenance of indigenous biodiversity.

The role of councils sits as a backdrop against which on-farm land-use practice occurs; but the way in which councils provide for indigenous biodiversity, and how this translates on farm, varies greatly around the country, and the enforcement of these policies can be lacking, making expectations even murkier.

Many initiatives are led or supported by government agencies, non-government funding bodies or communities, and result in voluntary actions on private land to protect and manage indigenous biodiversity. A sizable proportion of this effort happens on farm, such as the fencing of bush fragments, planting of riparian margins and control of pests. The number of Queen Elizabeth II Trust Open Space Covenants that protect areas of indigenous biodiversity on farm in perpetuity is often cited as a good indicator of positive on-farm biodiversity work (as at June 2016 there were 4626 protected open spaces across the country, covering 182,677 hectares).[6]

The pressure to do more

Maintaining the environment is becoming a key component of good farm management and a basic 'duty of care' expectation, including from export markets. There is increasing pressure, therefore, both domestically and internationally, to improve the management of natural resources, including indigenous biodiversity.

Increasing environmental resilience on farm and within catchments is critical. Not only does it sustain the long-term viability of the farm business by protecting natural assets and the capacity for production, it also maintains healthy and vibrant rural communities. The exploitation of natural resources beyond their natural limits threatens not only food and water security, but also economic security and the future of rural communities. Increasing environmental resilience requires maintaining and increasing farm-scale indigenous biodiversity.

New Zealand is party to several international agreements around maintaining biodiversity. From a conservation perspective, biodiversity is complex: it matters which species are covered by the agreements and where they are located. An important part of meeting international commitments is distinguishing between New Zealand's indigenous and endemic species and its exotic species.

In particular, it is important to identify invasive exotic species such as possums, rats, mustelids and weeds that degrade or destroy indigenous biodiversity and threaten the viability of production landscapes. This is not to say that exotic species are not valuable. Indeed, New Zealand's export economy is underpinned by introduced species, and pastoral landscapes are an important part of the cultural identity of many New Zealanders. Nevertheless, international pressures around biodiversity must be managed carefully.

Tools for managing biodiversity

Beyond protecting our remaining indigenous biodiversity, such as by excluding livestock, there are many avenues for enhancing biodiversity on farm. For example, the stability of erosion-prone soils on slopes and in gullies can be improved by the presence of woody vegetation. Soil conservation plantings have long been used for this purpose. But maintaining indigenous bush blocks or allowing indigenous gully vegetation to regenerate has the potential to deliver the same outcome with the added benefit of contributing to indigenous biodiversity conservation objectives.

Good management tools that can be used to improve biodiversity are available to farmers; for example, land evaluation and farm planning are two tools that are well established in New Zealand. Farm plans have long been implemented in various forms, having evolved from historical efforts targeted at soil and water conservation. Four land-based, farm-scale plans are in common use around New Zealand today: riparian plans, designed to deliver specific work programmes; nutrient management plans, designed to align on-farm actions and impacts with regulatory parameters; and land environment plans and whole farm plans, which provide detailed outcome-oriented work plans that address a wide range of issues on farm, as they apply to both the business and the underlying natural resources.

Additionally, and more generically, environmental management systems are commonly used to plan, audit and provide farm quality assurance systematically, based on a plan-do-check-act cycle. The various focuses of these farm plans have meant that biodiversity and the provision of ecosystem services are captured within the planning process to varying degrees but never as explicit goals.

A recent New Zealand case study tested the merits of incorporating an ecosystems approach into land evaluation and resource management by quantifying the ecosystem services provided by dairy-based agro-ecosystems on two contrasting types of soils. The case study found the approach to be a fundamental solution to the ongoing issue of environmental limitations.[7]

Expos and rural shows provide an
opportunity for learning about farm
management tools to increase biodiversity
and support farm sustainability.

The next step is to incorporate indigenous biodiversity considerations into the evaluation. At first glance, this may seem difficult, and indeed it will take a significant shift in current thinking and practice. It will be challenging, but combining the ecosystems approach with existing farm planning concepts provides the necessary pathway to integrate indigenous biodiversity into the farm system and couple the farm to the resilience of the wider catchment and community.

Moreover, the concepts underpinning current farm plans are well established, including evaluating on-farm assets, operating within constraints and setting targets for farm performance. In this sense, underpinning farm planning with an ecosystems approach is simply an evolution of existing practice.

Current practice can be extended to capture the full range of cultural, social, environmental and economic dimensions of the resilience of the farm system. More critically, taking an ecosystems approach provides the opportunity to recognise the contribution of indigenous biodiversity to every aspect of the farm business, including long-term resilience.

This recognition would help to shift the conversation on the ground from one of 'why?' to 'how?': how can farmers increase biodiversity to achieve farming and personal goals long term? Farm planning applies structure and cohesion to daily decision-making and links targets with the capabilities and conditions of the farm assets, meaning that the management actions required to effect change can be identified and implemented. This provides considerable opportunities for enhancing the condition of indigenous biodiversity, including reintroducing and restoring lost habitat.

What needs to change?

We suggest that approaches by central and local government to protect and encourage the maintenance of biodiversity on farm have failed largely because policies and programmes (where they exist) consider indigenous biodiversity in a manner that is divorced from other on-farm decisions around the management of resources and benefits to the farm systems.

For example, an emphasis solely on conservation objectives for a restricted number of high-value, significant areas is typical within many regions; however, it comes at the expense of considering the wider functional values of indigenous biodiversity on farm, such as erosion prevention, flood mitigation, nutrients attenuation, the health of animals and the well-being of people. Equally, the need for this emphasis is rarely communicated from the perspective of relevance to the landowner.

It can be unclear how individual actions on farm, or the farm itself, contribute to district or regional policies, or how these policies translate to necessary actions on farm. No farm operates in isolation; improving tools and processes that protect and manage indigenous biodiversity on farm provides another link between the farm and the wider community. Going further and increasing indigenous biodiversity actively on farm is a real opportunity to meet wider societal expectations of farming, reduce farming's environmental footprint, and improve farm resilience and the well-being of the wider community.

Maintaining biodiversity on farm needs to shift from being a 'nice-to-have' to becoming an integral part of farming systems. In addition, recognising that indigenous biodiversity contributes to a wide range of benefits spanning environmental, cultural, social and economic values necessitates a broadening of the conversation around managing biodiversity, an issue that New Zealand still grapples with and a long-standing debate that requires urgent national leadership to resolve.

The country also needs to recognise and value the 'rest' of the indigenous biodiversity — the species and habitats that are of lower conservation priority and, therefore, are deemed typically to have little or no value. They, along with those of high conservation value, need to be included in on-farm evaluation and day-to-day decision-making, as this inclusive approach is the key to building capacity and resilience on farm.

Bringing about change requires a shift in practice, and we suggest this shift needs to occur first at the very foundation of farming — land evaluation and farm planning — by focusing on the benefits flowing from nature that are consumed or used by humans to sustain or advance well-being. All elements of nature, including all natural resources, such as soil, water, vegetation and species, and the interactions between them (collectively referred to as 'natural capital'), contribute to the provision of ecosystem services. Such an approach allows a broader evaluation of the performance of the farm that goes beyond the production of commodities, capturing and evaluating all natural assets, including biodiversity, and the strengths, weaknesses and opportunities they provide.

Landowners around New Zealand have been practising land evaluation since the 1970s. We believe that the focus of land evaluation should be shifted from solely soils to the entire range of on-farm natural resources, including biodiversity. This broader evaluation can inform decision-making relating to land-use and management practices. In turn, actions can be targeted at specific outcomes, such as enhancing farming capacity, managing natural resources within environmental limits and maintaining resilience. This includes identifying opportunities to prevent further decline and enhance resources, such as replacing exotic shelter belts with indigenous tree species or undertaking wetland restoration.

A broader evaluation of the farm system would shift the focus towards the contributions the farm can make to a more diverse and multi-use landscape. The emphasis on production would be replaced with equal considerations of environmental, cultural, social and economic outcomes, meaning quadruple and multifaceted bottom lines — rather than the single economic bottom line on which many farmers appear to focus currently.

Chapter 13 —

An integrated approach to farming: Learning from mātauranga Māori

— *Estelle Dominati and Garry Watson*

H istorical natural resource exploitation has led to serious
challenges that confront New Zealand's rural communities.
These include land degradation, biodiversity loss, water
pollution and climate change, in addition to social issues such as poverty
and increasing inequalities. Such challenges contribute collectively
to reduced resilience and are relevant for everyone, particularly so in
rural communities, which must deal daily with the consequences of
inadequate land management.

New Zealand trades on its international reputation for producing safe and inexpensive food from a clean and green environment. The question of how best to use our land is very important if we want to address these challenges and find long-term solutions.

As a multicultural nation, New Zealand can play a major role in demonstrating to the world that engaging with indigenous cultures can inform the debate on the sustainability of natural resources. Those cultures with strong connections to the land, such as the Māori culture, have been operating holistic resource management for hundreds of years and can provide invaluable lessons on sustainable land management.

The need for a bicultural approach

New Zealand Māori have developed an intimate, holistic and inter-connected relationship with the natural environment with a rich knowledge base — mātauranga Māori — over hundreds of years of continuous occupation of Aotearoa. Mātauranga Māori is a consciousness, an enlightened state born of generations of connection, reliance, observation and dependency on the sustainable use of natural resources. Its foundation is genealogical: a whānau (family) connection with all living resources and the protection of their mana (integrity), their tapu (sacredness) and their mauri (life force).

This symbiotic relationship requires people to act first as guardians of the natural world and second as resource users. The benefits provided by the natural living world include cultural identity and spirituality and extend beyond amenity or utility values. The privileges and obligations that are recognised by Māori in the use and protection of all natural resources provide the foundation for individual as well as collective well-being, with no distinction drawn between tangata (people) and whenua (land). They are all one.

Māori knowledge systems are based on a strong sustainability ethic,[1] which is acquired by observing human interactions with the natural world and having to deal with the increasing pressure on, and depletion and degradation of, valued resources. The sustainability expertise underpinning mātauranga Māori has much to offer Western science research.

Many environmental issues, such as poor water quality and land degradation, have been attributed to agricultural practices, and the sector is now under pressure to demonstrate the sustainability of its practices to rural communities and consumers. In the past 30 years, more and more people have come to realise that you cannot have a strong economy without a healthy environment. That is, all types of resilience are strongly interrelated — an outlook that is evident in mātauranga Māori but largely lacking in Western science. So the question is, which approach best unites these two worlds and management practices?

Ecosystem-based management (EBM), which comes from Western science knowledge, has many similarities to mātauranga Māori. EBM is an example of a modern, integrative approach to natural resource management and can provide a range of tools for sustainable resource management to help with decision-making and ensure the delivery of outcomes across environmental, cultural, social and economic dimensions.[2] The integrated nature of EBM makes it seem the ideal candidate for engaging in environmental research with indigenous people, cultures and knowledge systems in which there are strong cultural connections to the land.

While guidelines and implementation strategies abound, the successful implementation of ecosystem-based management on the ground, however, has been slow. EBM revolves around the concepts of natural capital and ecosystem services. Natural capital refers to stocks of natural assets — or, in other words, all natural resources, from land to waterways to vegetation. Ecosystem services refer to the benefits that people obtain from the use of these natural resources.[3] These include being able to grow food and use resources, such as fresh water for drinking or recreation, wood, fuel and minerals. Benefits or ecosystem services also include the filtering of nutrients, mitigation of the adverse effects of climate change (e.g. flooding), the regulation of pests and diseases, and providing people with inspiration or a sense of place.

EBM rests on two main principles. First, natural resources should be maintained and enhanced to ensure the environment is healthy and functions well. It can therefore continue to provide long term all the things that people need, both directly, such as crop yields, and indirectly, such as flood mitigation. Second, land-use choice, intensity and management should operate within the capabilities and natural boundaries of both the land and the surrounding ecosystems to which they are linked. For example, all soils are different and soils have a finite capacity to retain nutrients. When reviewing land-use sustainability, limits and differences must be considered from the start.

The idea behind EBM is that resource management decisions and actions are based on a clear understanding of the priorities, benefits and impacts across the whole land-type/land-use system. Decisions should also rest on all the impacts, both positive and negative, of a change in management or land use on the full suite of benefits provided by a combination of land type and land use/management. For example, when planting trees such as poplars and willows for soil conservation, it is worth noting that those trees do not only prevent soil erosion; they also provide shade and shelter for animals, store atmospheric carbon, intercept rain and mitigate flooding, and are a food source for insects and birds.

Alignment of concepts between mātauranga Māori and EBM

While EBM is a good place to start with indigenous landowners, it does not address cultural values and how to enact them[4] and, despite EBM's seemingly ideal candidacy as the approach with which to integrate indigenous and Western knowledge systems, this integration has yet to be achieved in practice. As a result, there are few guidelines for how to implement it on the ground. This chapter begins this process, first by examining the link between mātauranga Māori and EBM, and second by providing an outline for a bicultural farm plan tool that puts this link into practice.

Everything is connected —

The ecological systems on which EBM is founded are complex and interconnected. Interactions between organisms and their environment take place constantly and everywhere at multiple scales and are critical to the resilience and regenerative capacity of ecosystems. It is because of this connectivity that a change in land use affects water and air quality, as well as all the other elements of natural or managed ecosystems. In EBM, therefore, degradation of natural capital stocks leads to negative impacts on the provision of all ecosystem services, which in turn decreases human well-being.

In mātauranga Māori, whakapapa (genealogy) links all living things. Natural ecosystems are born of Ranginui (sky father) and Papatūānuku (earth mother) and guided via all their children. Natural resources are derived from Io, the creation energy, and the atua (deities) that control and nurture these elements. The degradation of these resources, which have a kinship relationship to tangata whenua (people of the land), is considered sacrilegious. Shifts in the mauri of any part of the environment — for example, through use — would cause shifts in the mauri of immediately related components.[5] As a result, the whole system would eventually be affected. So it can be seen that mātauranga Māori goes one step further than EBM in demonstrating not only the connections between natural resources and people, but also the genealogical origins of these connections.

Four dimensions —

While the environmental and economic dimensions of EBM have been researched thoroughly, the cultural and social dimensions have been largely overlooked. The mauri model (an academic model for Māori health) takes an indigenous perspective using four key aspects: ecosystems (environmental), hapū (cultural), communities (social) and whānau (economical).[6]

Reciprocity —

To ensure that the use of natural resources provides benefits without any adverse effects, EBM aims to maintain or enhance the condition of natural resources through careful management. This is comparable to the notion of tauutuutu (or utu, reciprocity), which forms the basis of kaitiakitanga (guardianship of the land) in tikanga Māori. The concept of utu brings with it a privilege equal to its obligation, which rewards the kaitiaki (guardian, caregiver) with the mauri needed for him/her to thrive. Acting as a kaitiaki bestows mana on the guardian as it recognises and enhances the mana of the whenua and all natural resources. By taking good care of the land, the caregiver increases the mana of the land as well as their own mana. Again, while EBM remains utilitarian, mātauranga Māori embraces notions of stewardship of the land for reasons beyond economic return, which are based on a parental nurturing ethos.

Well-being —

Both Māori and EBM knowledge systems demonstrate strong links between the natural environment and human well-being. In EBM, the use of natural resources produces benefits for people that generate different types of well-being, from basic human needs such as food, water or shelter, to higher needs such as a sense of belonging, inspiration, self-actualisation or leisure. In mātauranga Māori, all living things are interconnected and interrelated. The principle of mauri can be used to understand connectivity and to measure sustainability and well-being. For Māori, impacts on well-being from the loss of connection to their land and natural resources can be measured using the Te Whare Tapa Whā model,[7] which views Māori communities and individuals as requiring a sound whare (house) in which to reside. The four corner poles (pou) of that whare are te taha hinengaro (psychological health), te taha wairua (spiritual health), te taha tinana (physical health) and te taha whānau (family health).

Intergenerational equity —
EBM emphasises the sustainability of human activities by arguing that future generations have the same right as the current generation to access abundant and healthy natural resources. It promotes shifting from models of economic growth to models of steady-state economy, where natural resources are not harvested to depletion but rather maintained and enhanced for other generations to be able to use.

Similarly, in mātauranga Māori intergenerational equity is an obligation born of whakapapa connections between nature and people, which drives the kaitiaki function, and in turn drives the need for sustainable land use within te ao Māori (the Māori world). Such protected or enhanced landscapes within Māoridom cannot be owned or sold but must be passed on to the coming generations, ensuring intergenerational equity. For Māori, the lands owns the people, not the other way around.

As such, the differences between mātauranga Māori and EBM can be seen as strengths, as together they demonstrate consideration of all dimensions of resilience and a unique way to link Māori and Pākehā values in New Zealand.

Farm plans as a tool for integration
For the past 20 years, farm plans have been the main tool for addressing resource management issues on New Zealand farms. As such, one critical

way to implement EBM and mātauranga Māori concepts is through a farm plan. Taking a more holistic approach to farm planning by bringing together business, environment and cultural goals allows for social, cultural, environmental and production values to be recognised and enhanced while focusing on the farm performance as a business.

Given that farm plans will remain — at least in the near future — an important tool for on-farm decision-making, it is important to consider how to improve them. The limitations in the current process can continue to be tackled and the process can evolve to capture emerging challenges. Farm plans can be used as vehicles through which to recognise the connectivity between all natural resources, their uses and their resilience.

Farm systems are already very complex, and with the ever-growing demand for more sustainable farming systems (see Chapter 10) the farm is where truly holistic and integrated approaches will need to be set in operation. In the past, issues such as nutrient losses, soil degradation or biodiversity loss have been dealt with in isolation from each other at both policy development and farm levels. Decision-making that ignores the full range of benefits provided by nature allows trade-offs between dimensions to be implicit, silent and unaccounted for.

In addition, Māori landowners face significant challenges in attempting to manage and administer their land. Māori freehold land comprises a little over 1.5 million hectares (5.6 per cent of New Zealand's land area) and is mainly situated in the central and eastern regions of the North Island. There is a significant area of Māori land in fragile natural environments such as wetlands, coastal areas, and margins of lakes and rivers. Māori agricultural land is usually of poorer quality because the most fertile land was sold or confiscated in the 1800s or early 1900s.[8] Therefore, it has been important for Māori landowners to reflect on the sustainability of their land use, while respecting cultural values and tikanga to deliver well-being for their people.

Many Māori landowners are looking to reconcile modern farming systems and practices with their cultural roots, cultural values and the way their ancestors used to care for the land. Therefore, there is a need to find ways to operationalise mātauranga Māori for natural resource management at the farm scale. The challenge for modern New Zealand, as a bicultural society, is to find ways to use land that build upon and learn from both Western knowledge and mātauranga Māori, where both value and knowledge systems are regarded as valid and equal and utilised to deliver sustainable land management for both Māori and Pākehā land.

Farm plan steps

Modern whole farm plans, such as the Beef + Lamb New Zealand Land and Environment Plan, follow several steps that could include the consideration of natural resources beyond land and economic value, encompassing environmental, social and cultural factors as well.[9]

Step 1: Goal setting —

The current farm planning process usually starts with goal setting. Here the objectives the landowners have for the farm, business and family are identified.

This phase of on-farm planning could be expanded to include wider goals such as long-term goals for whānau, hapū and iwi. This might include goals such as the desire to provide training for young people, the creation of attractive jobs to bring young people back to the land, the creation of open days for shareholders to learn about the land and its history, and the desire to regain access to culturally significant sites.

Because farms are not isolated but are part of catchments, other targets such as biodiversity or water quality targets, which operate at district, regional or national scales, should be considered. Thus, the goal-setting exercise should translate these broader outcomes to farm-scale targets that can be monitored and reported on.

Step 2: Stocktake of farm resources —

Next in the farm planning process is usually a stocktake of resources, including an inventory of existing capital in terms of quality and quantity. In the past this has been limited to describing the farm's land resources and built infrastructure.

In an integrated farm plan, this should be expanded to include descriptions of all farm assets including natural (e.g. soils, waterways, wetlands, vegetation, significant species), social (e.g. staff safety and well-being), cultural (e.g. access to sites of significance, use of cultural practices) and manufactured capital (e.g. farm infrastructure, roads). Some modern farm plans include analyses of the strengths and weaknesses of farm natural resources alongside analyses of the opportunities and threats.

The stocktake of farm resources should also include human resources and reflect on the connectivity between all resources: specifically, the impact of increasing the resilience of one part of the farm on the entire system.

Step 3: Definition of environmental, cultural and social boundaries —

This step is new to the farm plan process. Having carried out a stocktake of resources, landowners should next define environmental, cultural and social boundaries within which economic activity can occur.

This step may be informed by external policy, such as environmental regulations. Landowners already operate within a range of financial, social, cultural and environmental boundaries and consciously identifying and defining these boundaries at the farm planning stage will help them to be proactive in their farm management, as opposed to reactive.

This step is the opportunity for landowners to go beyond the minimum required to be compliant and establish farm management practices that follow their own personal goals and values. It is also the opportunity for Māori landowners to translate cultural values and tikanga into boundaries within which any economic activity can operate. Some boundaries will be defined at the farm scale, such as maintaining soil quality or the specific use of some part of the farm at certain times of the year for cultural reasons. Other boundaries will be defined at the catchment scale and relate to desired community outcomes (e.g. thresholds on nutrient losses and sediment) and consumer outcomes (e.g. practice and produce quality), while further boundaries may be defined at the national scale (e.g. greenhouse gas emissions to air).

Step 4: Assessment of the current performance in relation to goals —

The next step typically involves landowners assessing the inventory of resources and their current state in the context of personal values, stated goals and targets. This helps them to determine the extent to which those goals and targets are being met. This step identifies areas of the farm on which to focus, opportunities for the modification or introduction of new farming practices or the consideration of land-use changes for parts of the farm.

Under a more holistic EBM model, the processes within this step would remain the same, but as the farm boundaries have broadened to encompass social, cultural and environmental values, so too have the criteria for performance evaluation. At the beginning this will likely mean that a number of new farming practices or modifications will be brought in but will over time become integrated into and improve the existing farm system.

Step 5: Development of a work plan —

Building on the previous steps, a work plan that identifies and schedules the management actions is typically required to sustain or enhance resources to achieve the stated farm aspirations.

These goals will in turn be expanded to encompass the environmental, cultural and social targets.

Step 6: Monitoring and reporting —
The final step is the monitoring and reporting of the changes required to achieve farm management goals. Systems should be put in place to measure and track current outputs and performance towards goals using a range of carefully selected indicators identified both at the farm scale and beyond. This reporting will feed back into future goal setting.

The contributions of new farm planning
Integrating the EBM model into farm planning means including ecosystem services and different value types as part of the monitoring and reporting programme to enable long-term sustainability risks to be identified at an early stage in the process. Farmers will likely need to create potentially novel ways of measuring progress and impacts; for example, how to measure the cultural and social value of aspects of their farms. This may involve managing the protection of native species that hold cultural values or considering the damage that might have been done if unsustainable farming practices had continued.

Although this modified farm plan is at an early stage of conception, it provides a line of sight to a bicultural method of measuring progress towards greater sustainability on farm. If we consider the wider, more intangible aspects of farming, this could drastically change the way we farm — a change that would capture the greater value our farms can provide across the resilience dimensions.

New Zealand is fortunate to have at its disposal several knowledge systems, such as Western science with EBM and mātauranga Māori, on which to base approaches to sustainable land management. By utilising their rich history and heritage, New Zealand's rural communities have the potential to operate within cultural and social expectations, enhance farms' abilities to endure environmental or economic pressures, enhance the connectivity between nature and people, and demonstrate to the world the true uniqueness of our natural resources, products and people.

A classic scene from New Zealand's heartland, but
what will our rural landscapes look like in 20 years?

Conclusion —

The future of rural resilience in New Zealand

— Margaret Brown, Bill Kaye-Blake and Penny Payne

Throughout this book you've heard all about our rural communities: the current issues they are facing, the future changes that might affect them, the ways in which they are adapting and ways to think about their resilience.

At the start of this book we took you on a drive around rural New Zealand and looked at the changes on farm and in rural communities. This chapter takes that same drive, but 20 years in the future to see what our communities and farms could look like. Predicting what's to come is difficult, so on our drive we are drawing on the implications from our research into community resilience to answer this question.

We also ask a second question: How can rural communities shape their own futures? Each of our authors, who are mainly scientists or researchers, has presented some ideas based on their research into rural communities about how those communities can use their agency to shape their futures.

Driving to the future

As we drive through the future landscape of rural New Zealand, we'll see that some things are much the same as they are now. We will still pass through rural towns, but it is likely that some of the smaller ones will have continued to decline and will be consolidated into moderately sized towns. This amalgamation will be good for the moderately sized towns as they will be able to retain public facilities such as medical care, schools, banks, grocery stores and good internet access.

This consolidation could mean you travel longer distances between rural communities, but they would be larger 'hubs' when you reach them. People are likely to be attracted to these hubs because they will have sufficient residents to support a diversity of employment, people, lifestyles and activities. They will likely be more affordable than urban equivalents, as housing in the cities becomes more expensive and congested.

People who move to these hubs should be able to find meaningful non-agricultural occupations. This might be working with farms that have diversified into businesses beyond farming, such as tourism or land conservation, or even occupations that are not land-based.

For those who choose to stay behind in the rural areas despite the loss of their closest small towns, the increased distance to town will require rural households to be even more self-sufficient units than they are now, equipped for independence. Farm systems are likely to rely less on off-farm inputs such as feed, given that transport and additional farm inputs are likely to become more expensive. Digital technologies will be critical for alleviating rural isolation and providing on-farm labour and support for those who choose to stay. The impact of decline and distance could be reduced by self-driving cars and trucks that will allow farmers to spend their travel time doing other things as well.

Another critical consideration is how the consolidation of rural communities into larger rural hubs would affect rural infrastructure. Currently, rural infrastructure such as roading, water and rubbish collection is maintained by regional councils. These councils rely on a ratepayer base that in many rural areas is already struggling to cope. Maintaining large geographic areas with the money from a small population is just not viable in the longer term.

This problem will be magnified as these communities consolidate. With fewer people left in the more remote rural areas, who will be responsible for making sure that roads are still usable? It is also worth questioning whether maintaining these roads is necessary or even useful. These are big questions that New Zealand will be facing in the future; we will need to decide who is responsible for maintaining the rural built environment if it contains fewer and fewer occupants but continues to yield large volumes of agricultural products.

The future of farming

On our drive through the countryside of the future we will still see farms, but they will be different from how they are now. Climate change will mean more extreme weather events and new pests and diseases, resulting in greater vulnerability for monocultural and single-focus farming operations, so from the outset farms will need to spread risk by diversification. Having more revenue streams will provide people with more options. This might be the 'rural experience' farm stay, adding higher-value components to the business.

With finite resources available and an ever-growing population, agricultural enterprises will likely consider alternative products, inputs and processes. This might include insects and plants that are currently unused or viewed as pests or weeds. Diversification can be an effective way to increase resilience and will be critical for those who wish to remain on farm.

Risk will also need to be spread due to an increasingly stringent regulatory environment. More so than before, land managers will have a duty of care for environmental capital, including biodiversity, conservation, animal welfare, sustainability of production and so on. Farmers will have to demonstrate the effects of their land management practices on the wider ecosystem.

This will mean that those who follow the 'business as usual' of today, increasing the intensification and importing of feed stocks, will likely be forced out of business, as their model will not be competitive. (There will be other farmers who, operating sustainably in higher-value-added businesses, are producing less and earning more.) In addition, complying with regulation can be expensive. Stocking rates may be capped, waterways will need to be fenced, and fertiliser use will be restricted. Operating a viable, intensive farm system within these constraints will be difficult. Therefore, as we look out the car window, we are likely to see fewer livestock and single farms and a greater number of multifunctional farms with different types of land uses and entrepreneurial farm ventures.

All these changes will be made possible through use of better on-farm technologies. We will see sensors that enable the exact mapping of crops, fields and animals and their health, as well as decision-making software to help farmers decide when and where to water and how to use pesticides. These technologies will mean fewer farmers, too. If we stop on our drive and talk to farmers, we might find they have only two staff for a few thousand hectares, and they are likely to have more of a governance role. They might use artificial intelligence to help make the best decisions about farm management.

All of this technology assistance will also give consumers more of a view of what is happening in rural landscapes. They will be able to see where their food has come from with the scan of a barcode. They might learn that their steak is from a small farm near Te Kūiti that also farms rosemary and uses only natural fertilisers and pesticides. They will also have guarantees about how that animal was treated over its life. They may not even need to go the supermarket to get their food; these products could be selected online and delivered to their door.

The role of government

Changes are needed to allow New Zealand to meet its climate change adaptation and mitigation goals. These changes will have significant effects on rural community resilience; how these effects unfold depends in large part on how the government chooses to implement environmental policies over the next 20 years. If the government sets strict regulations on farming practices, prioritising environmental resilience, this could mean rapid changes for rural communities through farm closures, continued conversions and the appearance of more multifunctional landscapes. A prioritising of environmental resilience would mean potentially compromising economic and social resilience, at least in the short term. Cultural resilience would also be affected, in terms of rural communities' specific identities. Such changes would demonstrate how strongly the external dimension of resilience could affect the other dimensions of resilience.

As we have shown, resilience is also complex. The various sectors and regions will be affected differently, depending on how policies are implemented regionally or nationally.

Rural communities at the wheel

Despite the external nature of many of these changes, rural communities will, of course, play a part in determining their own resilience trajectories. A key message in this book is that rural communities have options; they are agents in this change.

One way for rural communities to prepare for these anticipated changes is to identify towns that could become hubs for the regions. This might be the largest rural town in the area or the most centrally located. Towns that are expected to be hubs can work to create an identity as emerging destinations for both local and overseas visitors.

Resilience hinges upon capability and capacity, which are dependent on investment — in roads, IT services, water systems, health and education — to attract and retain economically active population sectors. Towns that are tipped to become hubs need to be prepared to provide these critical services and infrastructure by working to create economies of scale and addressing issues in infrastructure requirements. Perhaps the government may recognise and acknowledge these towns as 'rural towns of significance' and give them additional funding so that they can build up their infrastructure to support both agriculture and tourism. The government might also consider putting in place policy or incentives to encourage more people to move from the cities to these hubs.

Towns that are likely to continue declining may need to consider their options carefully. This should include not over-investing in the community, working on improving current residents' quality of life, and focusing on acceptance strategies rather than countering strategies.[1] Attempting to counter population loss in peripheral rural towns is likely only to slow, rather than stop or reverse, population decline.[2]

Another option for preparing for the future is having a proactive agricultural sector that is driving and contributing to global food trends. This may include synthetic foods and high-value-added products that focus on creating cost-effective, sustainable, high-quality products. To enable this to happen, New Zealand will need to keep its reputation of being clean and green, as competition within this market will be strong. We also need to be able to demonstrate that we farm ethically, and embracing digital agricultural tools will be vital to this end. These will provide traceability and provenance, information about production and a guarantee that the product is what it claims to be. The adoption of digital technology will also help reduce the environmental impact of farming and could supplement on-farm labour, which is likely to be in short supply in the future.

An additional way for rural communities to increase their agency is through insisting that government analyse how policies will affect rural communities. That is, 'rural proof' their economic, social, cultural, institutional and environmental impacts. As we have seen throughout this book, rural communities can be strongly affected by external factors such as national- and regional-level policy decisions. Because so many of the environmental improvements needed must occur in rural areas, there may be a temptation to treat them as natural reserves, focusing on environmental priorities. Policy-makers also need to consider the implications for the people who choose to remain living in these locations.

These suggestions focus on being aware of the coming changes and contributing to them, rather than being subjected to them. We can be forearmed with knowledge of technological advances, prospective population changes and shifts in farming, and equip our rural communities as best we can. This will give rural actors an increased ability to control and mitigate undesired impacts and capitalise on new opportunities, such as diversifying their farm businesses.

Driving forces

Overall, we see elements of both continuity and discontinuity for rural communities. Things that we see as continuing are the strong social ties seen in rural areas; these might just be reconsolidated as towns go through phases of agglomeration. There will likely be continued changes in farm ownership, and possibly more corporate-owned and syndicate farms due to the financial pressures and risks for single-farm families. While there will also be ongoing environmental issues and pressure to deal with them, they may be resolved through continuing diversification in products, land uses and markets.

The elements of discontinuity or disruption we see are based around climate change and technologies. Climate change will necessitate changes in management, including managing risk. Technologies will provide options, while also changing what it means to be a farmer. These two big disruptors are occurring at a global scale, while the elements we have identified as likely to continue are operating largely at the regional or national scale.

Whatever happens will be a negotiated solution because of the number of options and because of the human agency; the future is not predetermined. The future, like the present, will emerge from all the different elements involved: individual choices, community choices, national policies and international trends.

The home stretch

Our drive through rural New Zealand has come to an end and we leave you with several key messages.

First, resilience is complex. You cannot measure resilience fully by separating its component parts, and communities can be resilient in different ways. This should not be underestimated; there is no 'silver bullet' (that we know of) for increasing resilience.

Second, resilience is more than local. National- and regional-level policies can have profound impacts on our rural communities. We need to remember this and consider all of the policy implications.

Third, people are resilient. Our rural communities will always be there; it is just a matter of what they will look like in the years to come.

Finally, people have options. Resilience trajectories are not set in stone or decided on solely by external parties. Looking back over the past 20 years, we can see how people on farm and in rural communities have built resilience into their systems and have adapted and changed their systems in the face of significant new opportunities and pressures. As a result, we anticipate that over the next 20 years people in rural communities will also be able to build their own resilience to accommodate the coming changes. In their own words, they take pride in their 'ability to influence change [and] participate in decision making', and in 'the community stability and support of its people'.

Kaitieke Horse Trek, King Country.

Notes

Introduction

1 Shamubeel Eaqub, *Growing Apart: Regional prosperity in New Zealand* (Wellington: Bridget Williams Books, 2014).

2 Paul Spoonley (ed.), *Rebooting the Regions: Why low or zero growth needn't mean the end of prosperity* (Auckland: Massey University Press, 2016).

3 Gabriele Bammer, *Disciplining Interdisciplinarity: Integration and implementation sciences for researching complex real-world problems* (Canberra: Australian National University E Press, 2013).

4 AgResearch, 'Resilient Rural Communities' (www.agresearch.co.nz/resilient-rural-communities).

Chapter 1 — On-farm changes that have affected rural communities in the past 20 years

1 Stats NZ, 'Livestock Numbers', in Environmental Indicators: New Zealand's environmental reporting series, 2017 (http://archive.stats.govt.nz/browse_for_stats/environment/environmental-reporting-series/environmental-indicators/Home/Land/livestock-numbers/livestock-numbers-archived-27-04-2017.aspx).

2 Birgit Boogaard, Bettina Bock, Simon Oosting, Johannes Wiskerke and Akke van der Zijpp, 'Social Acceptance of Dairy Farming: The ambivalence between the two faces of modernity', *Journal of Agricultural and Environmental Ethics* 24:3 (June 2011): 259–82.

3 Brent Irving, 'NZ Farm Ownership Trends and Models', a presentation at the Deer Industry Conference, May 2011 (www.deernz.org/sites/dinz/files/styles/Deer%20Industry%20FGM%202011%20Brent%20Irving%20rabobank.pdf).

4 Jacqueline Rowarth, 'Age is Only a Number', *idealog*, 1 February 2013 (https://idealog.co.nz/venture/2013/02/age-only-number).

5 Stats NZ, 'Change in Farm Numbers and Size', in Environmental Indicators: New Zealand's environmental reporting series (http://archive.stats.govt.

nz/browse_for_stats/environment/environmental-reporting-series/ environmental-indicators/Home/Land/farm-size-and-numbers.aspx).

6   Natalie Jackson, 'The Demographic Forces Shaping New Zealand's Future: What population ageing [really] means', *NIDEA Working Papers* 1 (May 2011), National Institute of Demographic and Economic Analysis, University of Waikato, Hamilton (www.waikato.ac.nz/__data/assets/pdf_file/0011/94619/2011-Demog-Forces-Revised2.pdf).

7   NIWA, *Annual Climate Summary: 2017*. Hamilton: NIWA National Climate Centre, 2018 (www.niwa.co.nz/sites/niwa.co.nz/files/2017_Annual_Climate_Summary_FINAL2.PDF).

Chapter 2 — Wairoa: Resilience and change

1   Wairoa District Council, *Wairoa 1998: A profile of the Wairoa district*. Wairoa: WDC, 1998.

2   LGNZ [Local Government New Zealand], 'Final voter turnout 2016' (http://www.lgnz.co.nz/nzs-local-government/vote2016/final-voter-turnout-2016/).

3   Geoff A. Wilson, '"Constructive tensions" in Resilience Research: Critical reflections from a human geography perspective', *The Geographical Journal* 184:1 (2018): 89–99.

4   Phil McManus, Jim Walmsley, Neil Argent, Scott Baum, Lisa Bourke, John Martin, Bill Pritchard and Tony Sorensen, 'Rural Community and Rural Resilience: What is important to farmers in keeping their country towns alive?', *Journal of Rural Studies* 28:1 (2012): 20–29.

5   Olivia J. Wilson, 'Rural Restructuring and Agriculture–Rural Economy Linkages: A New Zealand study', *Journal of Rural Studies* 11:4 (1995): 417–31.

6   Richard Bedford, Alun E. Joseph, Jacqueline Lidgard and Lex Chalmers, *Rural Central North Island: Studies of agriculture–community linkages: A report for the Ministry of Agriculture and Forestry* (Hamilton: Department of Geography, University of Waikato, 1999).

7   Organisation for Economic Co-operation and Development, *New Rural Paradigm: Policies and governance* (Paris: OECD, 2006).

8   Willie Smith, Christian Davies-Colley, Alec Mackay and Greg Bankoff, 'Social Impact of the 2004 Manawatu Floods and the "Hollowing Out" of Rural New Zealand', *Disasters* 35:3 (July 2011): 540–53.

9   Ann Pomeroy, 'Future Prospects in Rural Communities', a presentation to a business seminar held by the Geraldine Enterprise and Development Trust and Geraldine District Promotion Association, Geraldine, 28 September 1996.

10   Stats NZ, *Census Report 2018* (Wellington: Stats NZ, 2018).

11   Rosemary E. Ommer and Nancy J. Turner, 'Informal Rural Economies in

History', *Labour/Le Travail* 53 (2004): 127–57.

12   Tamar Diana Wilson, 'An Introduction to the Study of Informal Economies', *Urban Anthropology and Studies of Cultural Systems and World Economic Development* 39:4 (2010): 341–57.

13   Stats NZ, *Census Report 2018*.

14   Peter Buck, *Vikings of the Sunrise* (Christchurch: Whitcombe & Tombs Limited, 1964 [1938]).

15   Mason Durie, *Ngā Tai Matatū: Tides of Māori endurance* (Melbourne: Oxford University Press, 2005). Ian Pool, 'The Dismembering of the Maori Economy', in *Colonization and Development in New Zealand between 1769 and 1900: The seeds of Rangiatea* (Cham: Springer International Publishing, 2015), 253–83.

16   Colin C. Williams, 'Beyond the Commodity Economy: The persistence of informal economic activity in rural England', *Geografiska Annaler: Series B, Human Geography* 83:4 (2001): 221–33.

17   Lions International Wairoa, *Wairoa and District Lighthouse Lions Community Directory and Club Guide* (Wairoa, 2016).

18   Dave Grimmond, *The Economic Value and Impacts of Informal Care in New Zealand*, a report for Carers NZ and the NZ Carers Alliance (Wellington: Infometrics, 2014).

19   Michael Roche, 'Forestry', in Richard Le Heron and Eric Pawson (eds), *Changing Places: New Zealand in the nineties* (Auckland: Longman Paul, 1996), 160–8.

20   Michael K. Krausse, 'Impacts of Land-Use Change in Wairoa District', MAF Policy technical paper (MAF Policy, 1997).

21   Nathan Heath, Ian Millner, Erica Smith, Glen Lauder and Phillip Barker, 'Challenges Faced by Hill Country Farmers in New Zealand: The current issues, the state of research and what the future may hold', in Lance D. Currie and Ranvir Singh (eds), *Integrated Nutrient and Water Management for Sustainable Farming, Occasional Report No. 29* (Palmerston North: Fertiliser and Lime Research Centre, Massey University, 2016).

22   Michael Roche (ed.), *A Geographer by Declaration: Selected writings by George Jobberns* (Christchurch: Canterbury University Press, 2010), 75.

23   Heath et al., 'Challenges Faced by Hill Country Farmers'.

Chapter 3 — Talking to communities: How other small towns view their resilience

1   Rachael C. McMillan, 'Anticipating Subnational Depopulation: Policy responses and strategic interventions to regional decline' (master's thesis, University of Waikato, 2015).

Chapter 4 — The Sustainable Land Use Initiative: A community's response to an adverse event

1   EcoClimate, 'Costs and Benefits of Climate Change and Adaptation to Climate Change in New Zealand Agriculture: What do we know so far?' Prepared for Ministry of Agriculture and Forestry, April 2008.

2   NIWA, 'February 2004 North Island Storm (14 February 2004)', NZ Historic Weather Events Catalog (https://hwe.niwa.co.nz/event/February_2004_North_Island_Storm). 'Government Boosts Flood Aid to $30 million', *NZ Herald*, 4 August 2004 (https://www.nzherald.co.nz/nz/news/article.cfm?c_id=1&objectid=3582234).

3   Chris Ward, 'The Floods of 2004 — Looking Back', *RM Update* 16 (February 2005): 5 (http://www.maf.govt.nz/mafnet/publications/rmupdate/rm16/rm-february-2005.pdf).

4   Horizons Regional Council, *Storm: Civil emergency storm and flood report, February 2004*. Palmerston North: Horizons Regional Council, 2004.

5   Willie Smith, Christian Davies-Colley, Alec Mackay and Greg Bankoff, 'Social Impact of the 2004 Manawatu Floods and the "hollowing out" of rural New Zealand', *Disasters* 35:3 (July 2011): 540–53.

6   Andrew K. Manderson, Alec D. Mackay and Alan P. Palmer, 'Environmental Whole Farm Management Plans: Their character, diversity, and use as agri-environmental indicators in New Zealand', *Journal of Environmental Management* 82:3 (February 2007): 319–31.

7   Horizons Regional Council, *Review of Horizons Regional Council Sustainable Land Use Initiative* (2018): 34.

8   Margaret Brown, Simon Fielke, Alec Mackay, Tracy Nelson, Penny Payne, Tony Rhodes, Willie Smith and Jill Walcroft, 'It's Everybody's Business: Whole farm plans — a vehicle for implementing policy', a report for Horizons Regional Council/MfE (Hamilton: AgResearch, 2016). Horizons Regional Council, *Review*, 34.

9   Beef + Lamb New Zealand, 'Sheep and Beef Farm Survey', 2018 (https://beeflambnz.com/data-tools/sheep-beef-farm-survey).

Chapter 5 — A new framework to measure resilience

1   Simon Fielke, William Kaye-Blake, Alec Mackay, Willie Smith, John Rendel and Estelle Dominati, 'Learning from Resilience Research: Findings from four projects in New Zealand', *Land Use Policy* 70 (2018): 322–33.

2   William Kaye-Blake, Michael Dickson and Hannah Stapley, 'Applying the Concept of Resilience to an Integrated Research Programme'. Report prepared for the Our Land and Water National Science Challenge, November 2017,

AgResearch (www.ourlandandwater.nz/assets/Uploads/Applying-the-concept-of-resilience-to-an-integrated-research-programme-FINAL.pdf).

Chapter 6 — Creating an integrated perspective with modelling

1   This saying is attributed to Henri Theil, an econometrician, from his *Principles of Econometrics* (1971), but it seems to originate with Adam Przeworski, *Democracy and the Market: Political and economic reforms in Eastern Europe and Latin America* (Cambridge: Cambridge University Press, 1991).

2   William Kaye-Blake, Chris Schilling and Elizabeth Post, 'Validation of an Agricultural MAS for Southland, New Zealand', *Journal of Artificial Societies and Social Simulation* 17:4 (October 2014): article 5. Ronaldo Vibart, Iris Vogeler, Samuel Dennis, William Kaye-Blake, Ross Monaghan, Vicki Burggraaf, Josef Beautrais and Alec Mackay, 'A Regional Assessment of the Cost and Effectiveness of Mitigation Measures for Reducing Nutrient Losses to Water and Greenhouse Gas Emissions to Air from Pastoral Farms', *Journal of Environmental Management* 156 (2015): 276–89.

3   William Kaye-Blake, Chris Schilling, Ross Monaghan, Ronaldo Vibart, Samuel Dennis and Elizabeth Post, 'Potential Impacts of Water-related Policies in Southland on the Agricultural Economy and Nutrient Discharges', report to the Ministry for the Environment (Wellington: NZ Institute of Economic Research, 2013). This report and some other publications are available at www.agresearch.co.nz/resilient-rural-communities.

4   Sarah Baillie, William Kaye-Blake, Paul Smale and Samuel Dennis, 'Simulation Modelling to Investigate Nutrient Loss Mitigation Practices', *Agricultural Water Management* 177 (2016): 221–28.

Chapter 7 — Pathways to future resilience: The TSARA programme

1   For more information on the SDGs, see www.un.org/sustainabledevelopment/sustainable-development-goals.

2   For more details on the New Zealand part of TSARA, see Ronaldo Vibart, Matthew J. Smith, William Kaye-Blake, Matthew Brown, Kelly A. Stirrat and Alec Mackay, 'Targets for Sustainable and Resilient Agriculture (TSARA): A New Zealand perspective', AgResearch report for the TSARA project, 2017, as well as Ronaldo Vibart, Kelly A. Stirrat, William Kaye-Blake, Matthew J. Smith and Margaret Brown, 'Targets for Sustainable and Resilient Agriculture (TSARA): Indicators for the Sustainable Development Goals', AgResearch report for the TSARA project, 2018. These are available on the RRC website (www.

agresearch.co.nz/resilient-rural-communities) and the Our Land and Water National Science Challenge website (www.ourlandandwater.nz/resources-and-information/theme-and-programme-documents).

3   The complexity of resilience and the limits that communities face are discussed in Simon Fielke, William Kaye-Blake, Willie Smith and Ronaldo Vibart, 'Operationalising Rural Community Resilience: Framing indicators for measurement', Resilient Rural Communities report for AgResearch, 2017. It is available on the RRC website: www.agresearch.co.nz/resilient-rural-communities.

Chapter 8 — The resilience of Māori land use

1   Tanira Kingi, Liz Wedderburn and Oscar Montes de Oca, 'Iwi Futures: Integrating traditional knowledge systems and cultural value into land-use planning', in Ryan Walker, Ted Jojola, David Natcher et al. (eds), *Reclaiming Indigenous Planning* (Montreal, Kingston, London & Ithaca: McGill-Queen's University Press, 2013).

2   Waitangi Tribunal, *The Mohaka River Report 1992*, Wai 119 (Wellington: Brooker & Friend, 1992), 8.

3   Ibid., 9.

4   R. Joe, cited in 'Cultural Impact Report — Mohaka and Waikare Energy Development Investigative Study', prepared for the Section 30 Representatives by Toro Waaka, Ngāti Pāhauwera, 2007.

5   Public Act 2012 no. 30 (5 April), *Ngāti Pāhauwera Treaty Claims Settlement Act 2012* (www.legislation.govt.nz/act/public/2012/0030/latest/DLM3562516.html).

6   Ngāti Pāhauwera Deed of Settlement, 2010 (www.govt.nz/dmsdocument/2569.pdf).

7   Cordry Huata, in Waitangi Tribunal, *The Mohaka ki Ahuriri Report*, Wai 201 (Wellington: Legislation Direct, 2004), paras 24–31.

8   Elena Serfilippi and Gayatri Ramnath, 'Resilience Measurement and Conceptual Frameworks: A review of the literature', *Annals of Public and Cooperative Economics* (2018): 1–19.

9   Susan Cutter, Lindsey Barnes, Melissa Berry, Christopher Burton, Elijah Evans, Eric Tate and Jennifer Webb, 'A Place-based Model for Understanding Community Resilience to Natural Disasters', *Global Environmental Challenge* 18:4 (October 2008): 598–606.

10 J. M. Rendel, A. D. Mackay, A Manderson and K. O'Neill, 'Optimising Farm Resource Allocation to Maximise Profit Using a New Generation Integrated Whole Farm Planning Model', *Proceedings of the NZ Grasslands Association* 75 (2013): 85–90. Rendel et al., 'Valuing On-farm Investments', *Journal of NZ*

Grasslands 77 (2015): 83–8. Rendel et al., Moving from Exploring On-farm Opportunities with a Single to a Multi-year Focus: Implications for decision making, *Journal of NZ Grasslands* 78 (2016): 57–66.

Chapter 9 — Southland: An adapting landscape

1   New Zealand Dairy Statistics, 'New Zealand Dairy Statistics 2016–17', Livestock Improvement Corporation Limited and DairyNZ Limited (www.dairynz.co.nz/publications/dairy-industry/new-zeal;·nd-dairy-statistics-2016-17).

2   Keith D. Hamill and Graham B. McBride, 'River Water Quality Trends and Increased Dairying in Southland, New Zealand', *New Zealand Journal of Marine and Freshwater Research* 37:2 (2003): 323–32.

3   Lawrence McIlrath, Garry McDonald and Brian Bell, 'Southland Region: Economic impacts of water policy decisions workstream', in *Regional Economic Profile & Significant Water Issues*, a report for the Ministry for the Environment by Market Economics Limited, available at www.mfe.govt.nz (2013).

4   Dave Grimmond, Brian Bell and Michael Yap, 'Future Capability Needs for the Primary Industries in New Zealand', a report for the Ministry for Primary Industries by Infometrics and Nimmo-Bell (Wellington: MPI, 2014).

5   Jérémie Forney and Paul V. Stock, 'Conversion of Family Farms and Resilience in Southland, New Zealand', *International Journal of Sociology of Agriculture and Food* 21:1 (2013): 7–29 (19).

6   Denise Bewsell, Alec Mackay, William Kaye-Blake, Robyn Dynes, Oscar Montes de Oca Munguia and Margaret Brown, 'Collaborative Processes for Exploring Rural Futures: The exploring futures platform', *Rural Society* 26: 1 (2017): 48–68.

7   J. Doyne Farmer and Duncan Foley, 'The Economy Needs Agent-Based Modelling', *Nature* 460:7256 (2009): 685–6.

8   Sarah Baillie, William Kaye-Blake, Paul Smale and Samuel Dennis, 'Simulation Modelling to Investigate Nutrient Loss Mitigation Practices', *Agricultural Water Management* 177 (2016): 221–8.

9   Ronaldo Vibart, Iris Vogeler, Samuel Dennis, William Kaye-Blake, Ross Monaghan, Vicki Burggraaf, Josef Beautrais and Alec Mackay, 'A Regional Assessment of the Cost and Effectiveness of Mitigation Measures for Reducing Nutrient Losses to Water and Greenhouse Gas Emissions to Air from Pastoral Farms', *Journal of Environmental Management* 156 (2015): 276–89.

10 Iris Vogeler, Ronaldo Vibart, Alec Mackay, Samuel Dennis, Vicki Burggraaf and Josef Beautrais, 'Modelling Pastoral Farm Systems — Scaling from farm to region', *Science of the Total Environment* 482–3 (2014): 305–17.

11 Ronaldo Vibart, Alec Mackay, Andrew Wall, Iris Vogeler, Josef Beautrais and Dawn Dalley, 'A Farm-scale Framework to Assess Potential Farm- and Regional-

scale Implications of Removing Palm-kernel Expeller as a Supplementary Feed for Dairy Cows', *Animal Production Science* 57:7 (2017): 1336–42.

Chapter 10 — How will technology affect the fabric of rural communities?

1   Peter Alexander, Mark D. A. Rounsevell, Claudia Dislich, Jennifer R. Dodson, Kerstin Engström and Dominic Moran, 'Drivers for Global Agricultural Land Use Change: The nexus of diet, population, yield and bioenergy', *Global Environmental Change* 35 (2015): 138–47.

2   FAO, *World Livestock 2011: Livestock in food security* (Rome: Food and Agriculture Organization of the United Nations, 2011).

3   Nina Fedoroff, David Battisti, Roger Beachy, Peter Cooper, David Fischhoff, Carl Hodges et al., 'Radically Rethinking Agriculture for the 21st Century', *Science* 327:5967 (February 2010): 833–4.

4   Henning Steinfeld, Tom Wassenaar et al., *Livestock's Long Shadow: Environmental issues and options* (Rome: Food and Agriculture Organization of the United Nations, 2006) (www.fao.org/docrep/010/a0701e/a0701e00.HTM).

5   Johan Rockström, Will Steffen, Kevin Noone, Åsa Persson, F. Stuart Chapin, Eric Lambin et al., 'A Safe Operating Space for Humanity', *Nature* 461:7623 (September 2009): 472–5.

6   David Tilman and Michael Clark, 'Global Diets Link Environmental Sustainability and Human Health', *Nature* 515:7528 (November 2014): 518–22.

Chapter 11 — Entrepreneurship on New Zealand family farms

1   Cheree Morrison, 'The Purple Patch', *NZ Life & Leisure* (2016): 34–42.

2   Michael Mackay, Harvey C. Perkins and Stephen Espiner, *The Study of Rural Change from a Social Scientific Perspective* (Lincoln University: Department of Social Science, Parks, Recreation, Tourism and Sport, 2009).

3   Nicola Robertson, Harvey C. Perkins and Nick Taylor, 'Multiple Job Holding: Interpreting economic, labour market and social change in rural communities', *Rural Sociology* 48:4 (2008): 332–50.

4   Nick Taylor, Heather McCrostie Little and Wayne McClintock, 'Entrepreneurship in New Zealand Farming: A study of farms with alternative enterprises', in *MAF Policy Technical Paper* 97/7 (Wellington: Ministry of Agriculture, 1997).

5   Neil G. Gow, 'Farmer Entrepreneurship in New Zealand: Some observations from case studies', paper for 15th Congress — Developing Entrepreneurship Abilities to Feed the World in a Sustainable Way, in Campinas, Brazil, 2005.

6   Michael Mackay, Harvey C. Perkins and Nick Taylor, 'Producing and Consuming
     the Global Multifunctional Countryside: Rural tourism in the South Island of
     New Zealand', in Katherine Dashper (ed.), *Rural Tourism: An international
     perspective* (Newcastle upon Tyne, UK: Cambridge Scholars Publishing, 2014).
7   Michael Woods, 'Family Farming in the Global Countryside', *Anthropological
     Notebooks* 20:3 (January 2014): 31–48.
8   Anne M. Jervell, 'The Family Farm as a Premise for Entrepreneurship', in
     Gry Alsos, Sara Carter, Elisabet Ljunggren and Friederike Welter (eds),
     *The Handbook of Research on Entrepreneurship in Agriculture and Rural
     Development* (Cheltenham, UK: Edward Elgar, 2011).

Chapter 12 — Increasing indigenous biodiversity in farming landscapes

1   Susan Walker, Robbie Price, Daniel Rutledge, R. T. Theo Stephens and William
     G. Lee, 'Recent Loss of Indigenous Cover in New Zealand', *New Zealand Journal
     of Ecology* 30:2 (2006): 169–77.
2   Janet M. Wilmshurst, Atholl J. Anderson, Thomas F. G. Higham and Trevor H.
     Worthy, 'Dating the Late Prehistoric Dispersal of Polynesians to New Zealand
     Using the Commensal Pacific Rat', *PNAS* 105:22 (3 June 2008): 7676–80.
3   Marie A. Brown, R. T. Theo Stephens, Raewyn Peart and Bevis Fedder,
     Vanishing Nature: Facing New Zealand's biodiversity crisis (Auckland:
     Environmental Defence Society, 2015). Peter J. de Lange, Jeremy R. Rolfe, John
     W. Barkla, Shannel P. Courtney, Peter B. Heenan, Ewen Cameron, David A.
     Norton and Rodney A. Hitchmough, 'Conservation Status of New Zealand
     Indigenous Vascular Plants, 2012', *New Zealand Threat Classification Series 3*
     (Wellington: Department of Conservation, 2013).
4   *Department of Conservation Statement of Intent 2014–2018* (Wellington:
     Department of Conservation, 2014).
5   David A. Norton and Craig J. Miller, 'Some Issues and Options for the
     Conservation of Native Biodiversity in Rural New Zealand', *Ecological
     Management & Restoration* 1:1 (2001): 26–34.
6   QEII National Trust, 2017 (www.openspace.org.nz/Site/Publications_resources/
     Annual_statistics_maps_and_graphs.aspx).
7   Estelle Dominati, Alec Mackay, Johan Bouma and Steve Green, 'An Ecosystems
     Approach to Quantify Soil Performance for Multiple Outcomes: The future of
     land evaluation?', *Soil Science Society of America Journal* 80:2 (January 2016):
     438–49.

Chapter 13 — An integrated approach to farming: Learning from mātauranga Māori

1   Garth Harmsworth and Shaun Awatere, 'Indigenous Māori Knowledge and Perspectives of Ecosystems', in John Dymond (ed.), *Ecosystem Services in New Zealand: Conditions and trends* (Lincoln: Manaaki Whenua Press, 2013).

2   D. Scott Slocombe, 'Implementing Ecosystem-based Management, *BioScience* 43:9 (1993): 612–22.

3   Millennium Ecosystem Assessment, United Nations, 2005 (www. millenniumassessment.org/en/index.html).

4   Derrylea Hardy and Murray Patterson, 'Cross-cultural Environmental Research in New Zealand: Insights for ecological economics research practice', *Ecological Economics* 73 (2012): 75–85.

5   Rev. Māori Marsden and Te Aroha Henare, *Kaitiakitanga: A definitive introduction to the holistic world view of the Māori* (Wellington: Ministry for the Environment, 1992).

6   Te Kipa Morgan, 'Translating Values and Concepts into a Decision-Making Framework: Application of the Mauri model for integrated performance indicator assessment', National workshop, Roundtable on Sustainable Forests: A partnership for the future, Forest Products Laboratory, Madison, Wisconsin, USA, 5–7 September 2007.

7   Mason Durie, *Te Mana, Te Kāwanatanga: The politics of Māori self-determination* (Auckland: Oxford University Press, 1998).

8   Tanira Kingi, *Maori Landownership and Land Management in New Zealand* (Institute of Natural Resources, Massey University, Palmerston North, 2008) (https://dfat.gov.au/about-us/publications/Documents/MLW_VolumeTwo_ CaseStudy_7.pdf).

9   Estelle Dominati, Alec Mackay and Fleur Maseyk, 'Holistic Farm Planning – Using an Ecosystem Approach to Advance Farm Planning into the Future', Thirty-first Annual FLRC Workshop, Fertilizer & Lime Research Centre, Massey University, Palmerston North, 7–9 February 2018 (http://flrc.massey.ac.nz/ publications.html).

Conclusion — The future of rural resilience in New Zealand

1   Rachael C. McMillan, 'Anticipating Subnational Depopulation: Policy responses and strategic interventions to regional decline', master's thesis, University of Waikato, Hamilton, 2015.

2   Ibid.

About the authors

Dr Margaret Brown, senior social scientist in the People and Agriculture team at AgResearch, is based in Palmerston North. Margaret has a bachelor of education (Hons) and a PhD in education from Massey University. She has an extensive background in farm systems, as she co-owns and manages a mixed farming enterprise in Manawatū with her husband and son. Margaret currently leads the Resilient Rural Communities research programme under which this research was conducted, which looks at ways to co-design, construct and evaluate pathways that rural communities can use to build resilience capability.

Dr Vicki Burggraaf, scientist in the Farm Systems and Environment group at AgResearch, is based in Hamilton. Vicki grew up on a dairy farm in North Waikato, which ignited her interest in agriculture. Vicki's research focus is on understanding the interactions in farm systems, such as how climate, management, forages and genetics influence feed and animal production, animal health, profit and the environment. Vicki has worked with a range of farming systems, including dairy cow, beef and dairy goat enterprises.

Dr Estelle Dominati, senior scientist at AgResearch, is originally from Corsica, France. Estelle has a master's degree in agronomy and sustainable agriculture from SupAgro in Montpellier, France, and completed her PhD in ecological economics at Massey University in Palmerston North and AgResearch in 2012. Estelle's research has focused around economic valuation of ecosystems. More recently, Estelle has applied an ecosystems approach to resource management, looking at whole farm system analysis and optimisation. Estelle was the recipient of a Rutherford Foundation Postdoctoral Fellowship in 2012 and the Science New Zealand Early Career Researcher Award for AgResearch in 2017.

Dr Robyn Dynes is a farm systems scientist and is Science Impact Leader Farm Systems (Dairy) at AgResearch. Robyn has a bachelor of agricultural science (Hons 1) from the University of Canterbury (Lincoln College) and a PhD in ruminant nutrition from Lincoln University. Robyn leads research focused on future challenges and needs of the pastoral sectors dealing with multiple external pressures. She is from a pastoral and arable farming background and currently provides science perspectives supporting industry initiative across dairy, sheep and beef, and arable sectors.

Dr Kirsty Hammond was senior scientist in the Farm Systems and Animal Nutrition and Physiology teams at AgResearch in Palmerston North. The research focus of the team is to improve the efficiency of livestock production in New Zealand pastoral systems and develop animal production systems that are environmentally sustainable and ethically acceptable to consumers. Kirsty grew up on her family's dairy farm in Whakatāne and combined her love of animals with her love of farming in her bachelor of science (Hons) in animal science and physiology. She completed her honours in rumen development in deer and undertook a PhD in animal sciences, investigating methane emissions from ruminants fed fresh forage diets.

Bonny Hatami is project manager, Marine and Coastal Area (Takutai Moana) Act on the Ngāti Pāhauwera Takutai Moana applications, involving environmental project planning, funding proposals and delivery. Ngāti Pāhauwera will be the first to receive customary marine title under this act (2011), which replaced the Seabed and Foreshore Act 2004. She is a trustee of the Paroa Farm Trust and a member of Te Komiti Muriwai o Te Whanga — the Ahuriri Estuary Committee. She works on a variety of environmental and communication projects for the trust and liaises with local government and government agencies, sitting on various committees and working groups.

Dr William (Bill) Kaye-Blake, chief economist at PricewaterhouseCoopers New Zealand (PwC NZ), is based in Wellington. He has been studying food and agriculture for 25 years and is currently involved in interdisciplinary and international research on agri-food value chains, overseas consumer trends, and pathways for sustainable and resilient agriculture. Bill leads the economics consulting team in Wellington for PwC NZ and has contributed to consulting projects in Australia, China, New Zealand and the United States. He is also an honorary associate professor at Lincoln University and lectures in the executive MBA programme at Massey University.

Dr Alec Mackay, principal scientist at AgResearch, is based in Palmerston North. He has a bachelor of science (agricultural science) (Hons) and a PhD in soil science, both from Massey University, and is a fellow and past president of the New Zealand Society of Soil Science. He was awarded the Ray Brougham Trophy by the New Zealand Grasslands Trust for outstanding national contributions to pastoral farming industries. He leads research on refinements to land evaluation and farm systems modelling and planning tools. Current projects include adding ecosystem services to land evaluation processes and developing and testing a new generation of farm systems modelling capability to optimise the farm system within defined ecological boundaries.

Dr Michael Mackay, senior lecturer in rural and urban studies at Lincoln University, was previously senior policy adviser at DairyNZ, a lecturer in human geography at Lincoln University and a social scientist at AgResearch. He holds a PhD in human geography and a master's degree in applied science (tourism, rural change) from Lincoln University. Michael's research interests fall into the broad areas of human geography, rural studies, regional and small-town regeneration, social impact assessment, tourism research and critical qualitative inquiry.

Dr Fleur Maseyk, practice leader conservation science at The Catalyst Group, is an honorary fellow with the Centre for Biodiversity and Conservation Science at the University of Queensland. Over the past 20 years Fleur has worked for central and local government, a private ecological consultancy and an international conservation NGO, and as a postdoctoral research fellow. This has given Fleur broad-ranging experience in conservation and natural resource management at a strategic and policy level, and first-hand experience in on-the-ground realities. Fleur has great enthusiasm for linking science, policy and implementation, with a current focus on biodiversity policy, managing biodiversity in production landscapes, biodiversity offsets, and ecosystem service approaches to land management.

Tracy Nelson, science team leader in the People and Agriculture team at AgResearch, is based in Hamilton. She holds a master's degree in arts (human geography). Tracy's research interests cover understanding the adoption of new practices and technologies by people and on-farm diversification using qualitative research methods.

Penny Payne, social scientist in the People and Agriculture team at AgResearch, is based in Hamilton. She has a master's degree in community psychology and has studied at Victoria University of

Wellington, the University of Waikato and City University of Hong Kong. Current research areas include resilience, extension and education. Penny is currently evaluating extension programmes in climate change and biosecurity, targeting community, industry and schoolchildren. She also specialises in social network analysis, mapping relationships to explain and increase network resilience. Penny has worked with diverse audiences including rural communities, government, industry, not-for-profits, schoolchildren and regulatory organisations.

Dr John Rendel, scientist at AgResearch in Mosgiel since 2010, specialises in farm systems modelling and design. Prior to that he was a scientist at Landcorp working on farming breeding programme design and farm systems modelling. John has a PhD in quantitative genetics from Massey University. He is interested in applying optimisation tools to pastoral farming not only to identify the optimum but also to paint a picture of what the farm system may look like in order to understand how the farm influences the supply chain and vice versa. This approach can then be extended to understand how groups of farms may work together, especially in a value/supply chain context.

Dr Bruce Small, senior scientist at AgResearch, has expertise in environmental ethics, green technologies and technology futures. His PhD in social psychology and philosophy of ethics was a mixed-methods, empirical ethics thesis examining scientists' moral role in an increasingly high-tech society. Bruce also holds a master's degree in industrial and organisational psychology (Hons 1) from the University of Waikato.

Dr Willie Smith is a geographer, and holds an MA from the University of Aberdeen and an MSc and PhD from McGill University in Montreal. Willie's career includes extensive periods as an academic at universities in Canada, Africa and New Zealand, working as a science adviser at the Science Council of Canada in Ottawa and as a contractor on policy research. Willie's research focuses on public policy, particularly science and technology policy; farmers' decision-making; land-use change; and natural hazards. He has held appointments on national advisory committees, including the Committee for the National Science Strategy for Sustainable Land Management.

Dr Ronaldo Vibart, scientist in the Farm Systems team at AgResearch, has been based in Palmerston North since 2010. He obtained his master's degree and PhD at North Carolina State University in the US before moving to New Zealand in 2008. Current research areas include agricultural systems behaviour and the biophysical, social and environmental implications of integrating new technologies into the pastoral agribusiness sector. He is also involved in modelling the effects of farm- and regional-scale land-use changes on socio-economic and environmental outcomes, as well as aspects of ruminal microbial biomass associated with methane emissions and nitrogenous excretions from ruminants grazing temperate grasslands.

Garry Watson, chairman of Nga Uri o te Ngahere Trust, is of Ngāitai [Tainui]/Tūhoe descent. Garry is the research director of the trust, with 35 years' experience working with indigenous communities internationally and in environmental research. He specialises in the use and application of mātauranga Māori and rongoā Māori in ecosystem restoration and protection. The trust co-owns Trinity Bioactive and Garry has led a number of research programmes investigating the bioactive properties of New Zealand's native plant species. He leads the Vision Mātauranga collaboration established between AgResearch and the trust.

Acknowledgements

Margaret, Bill and Penny would like to acknowledge and thank their colleagues for taking their respective research findings and writing about them in the popular style of this book. It is no mean feat for scientists to summarise their research in this way, and their efforts to share their knowledge are very much appreciated.

We also wish to acknowledge and thank all the individuals, groups and rural communities who gave freely of their time to be involved in the research which formed the basis for *Heartland Strong*. We are very grateful for the time you spent with us, for the personal stories and knowledge you shared and for your writing and review of the chapters. It has truly been a community effort and we hope that our joint insights and learnings will help other rural communities to consider their own resilience and the options they might have to change, thrive and be strong.

Index

Numbers in **bold** indicate illustrations

First published in 2019 by Massey University Press
Private Bag 102904, North Shore Mail Centre
Auckland 0745, New Zealand
www.masseypress.ac.nz

Design by Megan van Staden
Cover photographs: Front above: Stuff Media; front below: Photo New
Zealand; back (from top): iStock, Photo New Zealand and Shutterstock.

A catalogue record for this book is available from the National Library
of New Zealand

Printed and bound in China by Everbest Printing Investment Ltd

ISBN: 978-0-9951095-9-9
eISBN: 978-0-9951135-7-2